Leaving Fear at Heaven's Gate

Leaving Fear at Heaven's Gate

GOD'S GRACE: THE ANSWER FOR ANXIETY

Theresa Ellison

Xulon Press Elite
555 Winderley Pl, Suite 225
Maitland, FL 32751
407.339.4217
www.xulonpress.com

© 2023 by Theresa Ellison

All rights reserved solely by the author. The author guarantees all contents are original and do not infringe upon the legal rights of any other person or work. No part of this book may be reproduced in any form without the permission of the author.

Due to the changing nature of the Internet, if there are any web addresses, links, or URLs included in this manuscript, these may have been altered and may no longer be accessible. The views and opinions shared in this book belong solely to the author and do not necessarily reflect those of the publlsher. The publisher therefore disclaims responsibility for the views or opinions expressed within the work.

Unless otherwise indicated, Scripture quotations taken from the King James Version (KJV) – *public domain.*

Paperback ISBN-13: 978-1-66288-772-7
eBook ISBN-13: 978-1-66288-773-4

All Scriptures are taken from the KING JAMES
VERSION (KJV): KING JAMES VERSION,
public domain.

Author's website:
www.blessmyblog.com

Table of Contents

Day 1. Fear is Finished 1
Day 2. Fear is Found in the Garden 9
Day 3. A Plan for Painful Emotions 12
Day 4. Condemnation Cancelled. 25
Day 5. Cages Constructed With Lies 25
Day 6. Comfort is in a Covenant. 29
Day 7. The Cup of Grief or Grace 35
Day 8. Does Healing Really Happen Today?. 38
Day 9. Treating Symptoms Without the Savior . . 38
Day 10. Get Off the Hamster Wheel 50
Day 11. What About Will Power? 54
Day 12. Two Choices. 62
Day 13. The Changing World 72
Day 14. Is Worry Worth a Badge?. 78
Day 15. Angels 83
Day 16. A Heart of Peace 89
Day 17. Weary? Wear the Right Yoke 93

Day 18. The Traveling Companions of Trouble 95
Day 19. Withered and Weak 99
Day 20. Walls of Protection 105
Day 21. Safe With Your Savior 108
Day 22. The Psalm of Protection 113
Day 23. Complete in Christ 117
Day 24. Christ Esteem 122
Day 25. Difficult Decisions 125
Day 26. Torment in the Night 133
Day 27. Sleep Encounters 136
Day 28. A Destination Wedding 144
Day 29. The Wedding Without Fear 147
Day 30. Are Grief and Fear Weaving a Wall
 Around Your Heart? 153
Day 31. Work Doesn't Define Your Worth 156
Day 32. Believe and Receive Healing
 Like Hezekiah 164
Day 33. Don't Fear Your Failure 169

About the Author 173
Further Reading 175

Leaving Fear at Heaven's Gate

An Introduction to Healing Grace

Fear is captivating the minds of God's people. Rather than living with the promise of a sound mind, believers are putting up with needless anxiety. Pounding on professional doors instead of boldly approaching the throne of God, Christians have dismissed an important truth. They have an inheritance of peace. Saved from sin but forsaking a sound mind, they are missing out on God's best.

> *In whom also we have obtained an inheritance, being predestined according to the purpose of him who worketh all things after the counsel of his own will. (Eph. 1:11)*

> *For God hath not given us the spirit of fear; but of power, and of love, and of a sound mind. (2 Tim. 1:7)*

There is a new and living way to get the help you need. It's called grace. You won't need an appointment. Everything is provided for. Get ready to receive. Jesus opened Heaven's gate to a glorious inheritance. What is included in His will? Healing for every type of emotional pain. Unlike the conventional approach to treating anxiety, this plan won't fail.

> *Having therefore, brethren, boldness to enter into the holiest by the blood of Jesus,* ***By a new and living way****, which he hath consecrated for us, through the veil, that is to say, his flesh. (Heb. 10:19-20) (Emphasis, mine)*

> *I am the Lord that healeth thee. (Ex. 15:26)*

There is a big difference between secular counseling and God's grace. Fear is not removed through medication or mastering mindfulness. Prescriptions and psychological techniques manage symptoms but fail to address the root cause. Obtaining freedom from fear is found only in Jesus Christ. This is not one of those *it's too good to be true* speeches. It is all possible because the Father loves you. He provides the abundant life you are seeking. There is no reason to put up with an enemy robbing your peace and plastering your mind with anxiety.

An Introduction To Healing Grace

> *The thief cometh not, but for to steal, and to kill, and to destroy: I am come that they might have life, and that they might have it more abundantly. (Jn. 10:10)*

There are too many believers living with anxiety. While there are many reasons they live compromised lives, a common cause is ignorance. Inadequate understanding of God's Word keeps believers in bondage.

> *My people are destroyed for lack of knowledge. (Hos. 4:6)*

> *Then said Jesus to those Jews which believed on him, If ye continue in my word, then are ye my disciples indeed; And ye shall know the truth, and the truth shall make you free. (Jn. 8:31-32)*

Sadly, believers haven't fully comprehended that fear lost its power and is a mere tool of the devil. Fear remains dormant until doubt segues into the soul. Doubt second guesses God. Listening to the roars of the lion instead of trusting in the Father, backs people into walls of helplessness. What should be done? Don't permit the devil to open his toolbox of lies and get his foot into the doorway of your mind.

> *Be sober, be vigilant; because your adversary the devil, as a roaring lion, walketh about, seeking whom he may devour. (1 Pet. 5:8)*

Before fear finds the welcome mat and sits on your sofa, turn to the throne of God. Reigning above this enemy, Christ Jesus shut Heaven's gate to fear. Where is fear now? Under His feet. There is more good news, Jesus has granted you the same authority over it. Join Jesus and tread upon this distress rather than letting it to climb into your mind.

> *For he hath put all things under his feet. (1 Cor. 15:27)*

> *Thou shalt tread upon the lion and adder: and the young lion and the dragon shalt thou trample under feet. (Ps. 91:13)*

Fear has no right trespassing into your territory. Your heart is an extension of the Kingdom of God. Therefore, shut your temple door on fear and rest in God's saving grace. Why miss out on the gift of His peace?

> *Neither shall they say, Lo here or, lo there! for, behold, the kingdom of God is within you. (Lk. 17:21)*

An Introduction To Healing Grace

> *Know ye not that ye are the temple of God, and that the Spirit of God dwelleth in you? (1 Cor. 3:16)*

> *Now the Lord of peace himself give you peace always by all means. The Lord be with you all. (2 Thess. 3:16)*

Leaving Fear at Heaven's Gate will encourage people suffering from anxiety to receive their inheritance of peace through Christ Jesus. Fear will find its gate shut as you recognize the door to peace is dwelling in your midst.

> *Say to them that are of a fearful heart, Be strong, fear not: behold, your God will come with vengeance, even God with a recompence; he will come and save you. (Is. 35:4)*

Dedication

This book is dedicated to the Heavenly Father. Due to His passionate love; fear relinquished its power over us. Peace is now possible because His Son, Christ Jesus, walked this earth for 33 years to provide the way into His Father's Kingdom. No other, would willingly, be crucified and raised from death, to pay for our sins. His grace has swung the gate of Heaven open to an abundant inheritance. Therefore, these 33 readings are committed to reflecting our Father's heart. May His Word be what is relished within each page of this book. All praise goes to the Father, Son, and Holy Spirit for freeing us from fear.

Day 1
Fear is Finished

Fear

Fear is a response to a real threat. Flight, fight, or freeze are inborne defense mechanisms serving to secure our safety. People may differ in their reactions to impending harm but with the same goal intended; to protect themselves from danger. If a man pointing a gun is approaching you, it is a natural response to either flee, fight back, or find your body immobilized. However, some fears are not reality based but live in the imagination. This type of fear is referred to as anxiety. Anxiety is the culprit of changing common people into mental health clients.

Anxiety

Anxiety is maintaining a state of fearfulness in the absence of real harm. Fear turns into a futuristic mindset and births a steady stream of worrisome thoughts. This perceived fear is like living in a fantasy world filled with frenzy. The imagination runs wild, holding hands with negative outcomes. Many clients describe it as a hamster wheel. This ongoing thought process creates a dysfunctional belief system. People run with their fears believing they hold truth and validity. This is dangerous because fear negatively impacts our spiritual, physical, and emotional well-being.

Whatever fear is afflicting you; don't you agree it is time to draw a line in the sand? Your heavenly Father felt the same way, so He posted a cross, establishing a line between the enemy of our soul and His peace.

Fear Faces the Finish Line

The death and resurrection of Christ Jesus has finished off our enemies. Sin and Satan lost the race in keeping us apart from the Father's Kingdom. Fear can only view us from a distance, for the Prince of Peace has brought us over to the winning side. We will never look at fear the same way again when we see it through the eyes of Christ.

> *When Jesus therefore had received the vinegar, he said, It is finished: and he bowed his head, and gave up the ghost. (Jn. 19:30)*
>
> *To the praise of the glory of his grace, wherein he hath made us accepted in the beloved. In whom we have redemption through his*

> *blood, the forgiveness of sins, according to the riches of his grace. (Eph. 1:6-7)*
>
> *As far as the east is from the west, so far hath he removed our transgressions from us. (Ps. 103:12)*
>
> *For unto us a child is born, unto us a son is given: and the government shall be upon his shoulder: and his name shall be called Wonderful, Counsellor, The mighty God, The everlasting Father, The Prince of Peace. (Is. 9:6)*

This victory involves a great inheritance. It grants the same power which raised Jesus from the dead to live in us. We share in His divine nature through the promises in His written Word.

> *According as his divine power hath given unto us all things that pertain unto life and godliness, through the knowledge of him that hath called us to glory and virtue: Whereby are given unto us exceeding great and precious promises: that by these ye might be partakers of the divine nature, having escaped the corruption that is in the world through lust. (2 Pet. 1:3-4)*

Don't underestimate this divine power. Through the Holy Spirit we can cast aside anything that comes against His promises. This means we do not have to accept every thought entering our minds. We are God's children living on the side of truth. Lies delivering fears have no right synchronizing with our souls.

> *Casting down imaginations, and every high thing that exalteth itself against the knowledge of God and bringing into captivity every thought to the obedience of Christ. (2 Cor. 10:5)*

The obedience mentioned in the verse above is not our own, but the obedience of Christ Jesus on the cross. Therefore, with the work done, and the battle won, we walk in victory over fear. Our role is to choose our thoughts carefully. Invite only thoughts aligning with the Word and cast aside anything involving the evils of this world. If unsure of what the mind of Christ is, read the Holy Bible.

> *If ye then be risen with Christ, seek those things which are above, where Christ sitteth on the right hand of God. Set your affection on things above, not on things on the earth. (Col. 3:1-2)*

God Dwells in You

Fear and Christ cannot coexist. God is good and fear is evil, period. Fear is not our friend for it is an enemy of God. We need to know when fear is prowling around our premises. Many recognize fear as only a panicky feeling or the clammy hands it creates. They may assume this is normal and put up with it. Fear wants us to grow accustomed to its symptoms so it can bring more suitcases into our lives. We should never allow anxiety to put its name on our mailbox. We need to erect a privacy fence and post no trespassing signs before it invades our property. A good daily practice is to examine who is entertaining our thoughts. Let us become doorkeepers over our minds. Anxiety starts with a simple thought. When it rings the doorbell, reject the basket welcoming you to the neighborhood. The welcome wagon of evil just wants to roll you out of God's presence. Think of it this way, a home filled with love doesn't mingle with evil. Evil will taint our thinking with gloom and doom, whereas love provides us with a sound mind.

> *Whosoever shall confess that Jesus is the Son of God, God dwelleth in him, and he in God. And we have known and believed the love that God hath to us. God is love; and he that dwelleth in love dwelleth in God, and God in him. Herein is our love made*

perfect, that we may have boldness in the day of judgment: because as he is, so are we in this world. There is no fear in love; but perfect love casteth out fear: because fear hath torment. (1 Jn. 4:15-18)

For God hath not given us the spirit of fear; but of power, and of love, and of a sound mind. (2 Tim. 1:7)

Fear Finds an Entry

How then does fear find the walkway into our souls? We surely don't want it on our welcome mat. The only port of entry fear has into our life is through the fabrication of lies. The devil, who is the liar, hopes we give access for him to cross the threshold into our lives. He does this by dropping a deceiving thought into our minds. It may look so polished we believe it is our own. The devil hopes we don't see his disguise. If we aren't operating with the mind of Christ, discerning good from evil, we can take a bite into his anxious apple. If we do, we partake in his evil schemes. We can be wise to his ways by immersing our minds in the Word.

A big indicator the devil has made privy into our minds is the absence of peace. Christ Jesus always leads with peace and distress is derived from the devil. Be mindful, we live amid two kingdoms, with a strong gate between them. It is God's will that the gate of our minds remains shut to Satan's domain. May we exercise our free will appropriately.

> *Ye are of your father the devil, and the lusts of your father ye will do. He was a murderer from the beginning, and abode not in the truth, because there is no truth in him. When he speaketh a lie, he speaketh of his own: for he is a liar, and the father of it. (Jn. 8:44)*

> *But I fear, lest any by any means, as the serpent beguiled Eve through his subtilty, so your minds should be corrupted from the simplicity that is in Christ. (2 Cor. 11:3)*

In closing, Christ Jesus has left fear behind the finish line. Therefore, when anxiety knocks on your heart, lock it out. Greater power is within you than the fear outside heaven's gate.

> *And when he was demanded of the Pharisees, when the kingdom of God should come, he answered them and said, The kingdom of God cometh not with observation: Neither shall they say, Lo here! or, lo there! for, behold, the kingdom of God is within you. (Lk. 17:20-21)*

Ye are of God, little children, and have overcome them: because greater is he that is in you, than he that is in the world. (1 Jn. 4:4)

What time I am afraid, I will trust in thee. (Ps 56:3)

Day 2
Fear Is Found in the Garden

Back to Genesis

Going back to the beginning, Genesis reveals that fear waltzed into the Garden of Eden after Adam and Eve disobeyed the Lord. Eating the fruit from the Tree of Knowledge opened the door to death and all its companions. Separated from the perfect love of the Father, fear replaced perfect peace. Simply stated, fear was sourced out of sin.

> *And they heard the voice of the LORD God walking in the garden in the cool of the day: and Adam and his wife hid themselves from the presence of the LORD God amongst the trees of the garden. And the Lord God called unto Adam, and said unto him, Where art thou? And he said, I heard thy voice in the garden, and **I was afraid**, because I was*

> *naked, and I hid myself. And he said, who told thee that thou wast naked? Hast thou eaten of the tree, whereof I commanded thee that thou shouldest not eat? (Gen. 3:8-11) (Emphasis mine)*

Before you become depressed due to this obstruction of peace, peer into the Father's gracious plan. While sin threw Adam and Eve out of harmony with the Father, He already had a resolution in place. His love had them covered. However, Adam and Eve did not consult the Father for His help, but independently devised their own means of remedy. Discovering the covering of God's glory had been removed, they tried to replace their nakedness with leaves.

> *And the eyes of them both were opened, and they knew that they were naked, and they sewed fig leaves together, and made themselves aprons. (Gen 3:7)*

The futile attempt to hide their impurity was inept, therefore the Father replaced their leaves with animal skins. The exchange demonstrated how the payment for sin required blood. While no human held power to purify sin; the son of God did. Genesis 3:21 is the foreshadow of the cross.

Fear Is Found In The Garden

> *Unto Adam also and to his wife did the LORD make coats of skins and clothed them. (Gen. 3:21)*

Obviously, we aren't wearing animal skins today to cover our sins. Jesus' sacrifice offers redemption to us and to all those who believe in Him. There is no fear of judgment since sin's penalty has been paid by the blood of Jesus. Next time you feel judged, condemned or afraid of being less than worthy, remember you are covered by the Father's love. Your acceptance in Christ Jesus is secure and cannot be removed. You don't have to hide from God since you are hidden in Christ's redemption. If you aren't convinced the Father cares about your fear, go back to Genesis and see how God took care of it as soon as it entered Adam and Eve's world. Surely, He has not changed and will do the same for you.

> *For God so loved the world, that he gave his only begotten Son, that whosoever believeth in him should not perish, but have everlasting life. (Jn. 3:16)*

> *For ye are dead, and your life is hid with Christ in God. (Col. 3:3)*

Day 3

A Plan for Painful Emotions

I have developed treatment plans with clients for a myriad of problems. Small steps and achievable goals were in place. It appeared the clients were off to a good start. However, while the inspiration was initially fresh, as the weeks went on something drained their motivational tanks. Old habits and fleshly desires interfered, causing disheartening setbacks. Revising treatment plans only deleted their defeat on paper. Personal failure was now etched upon their hearts. Without permission from the client to include Jesus Christ and His Word into their care, the plan plummeted.

> *Blessed is the man that walketh not in the counsel of the ungodly, nor standeth in the way of sinners, nor sitteth in the seat of the scornful. But his delight is in the law of the Lord; and in his law doth he meditate day and night. (Ps. 1:1-2)*

I am convinced the secular approach to counseling cannot promote lasting change. Working within the scope of human efforts and knowledge is like containing a whirlwind. Deliverance can't be grasped. When the force of fear destroys the inner being, the search for a solution must come from outside of oneself. Reach for genuine help. Psychology is a science, not a Savior.

> *When your fear cometh as desolation, and your destruction cometh as a whirlwind; when distress and anguish cometh upon you. (Prov. 1:27)*

When you have come to the end of yourself, stretch forth your hand. Your Savior Jesus Christ is waiting to heal your anguish. He doesn't do things halfway. Wholeness is awaiting. You are no different from the man Jesus encountered with a withered hand. The disabled man had nobody to help him. His hand's condition must have hindered his daily functioning. The moment he looked to Jesus; his deteriorating life turned prosperous. Who wouldn't want the Savior of the world to treat their condition?

> *Then saith he to the man, stretch forth thine hand. And he stretched it forth; and it was restored whole, like as the other. (Matt. 12:13)*

Stop Your Search

Stop your search for treatment. Spend your time meditating upon Scripture. The Word will drive out fear as you draw near to Christ Jesus. Let the Word discard the barriers of unbelief so you can receive His hand of deliverance.

> *All scripture is given by inspiration of God, and is profitable for doctrine, for reproof, for correction, for instruction in righteousness. (2 Tim. 3:16)*

> *For I the Lord thy God will hold thy right hand, saying unto thee, Fear not; I will help thee. (Is. 41:13)*

> *Then said the Lord unto me, Thou hast well seen: for I will hasten my word to perform it. (Jer. 1:12)*

Barriers of Unbelief

As a counselor I continually looked for barriers inhibiting success. The only barrier to receiving healing of the mind or body is unbelief. The problem certainly is not with Jesus nor in what He is trying to give us. No, it is our doubts building walls between Heaven's resources and our receiving them. Relish in His Word. The barrier is removed by hearing the Word of God. Stop your search, submerge yourself with Scripture and receive healing grace for your fearful heart today.

> *Jesus said unto him, If thou canst believe, all things are possible to him that believeth.*
>
> *And straightway the father of the child cried out, and said with tears, Lord, I believe; help thou mine unbelief. (Mk. 9:23-24)*
>
> *So then faith cometh by hearing, and hearing by the word of God. (Rom. 10:17)*

Day 4

Condemnation Cancelled

If you are experiencing the exchange of cutting words, please continue reading this message. When the blood runs down to your toes after hearing someone berate you, it is pertinent to respond in Christ's power. Condemnation kills but the Spirit gives life. There is much power in the tongue. We can speak life or death. Be careful you aren't siding with the devil and damage your own soul.

> *There is therefore now no condemnation to them which are in Christ Jesus, who walk not after the flesh, but after the Spirit. For the law of the Spirit of life in Christ Jesus hath made me free from the law of sin and death. (Romans 8:1-2)*
>
> *Death and life are in the power of the tongue: and they that love it shall eat the fruit thereof. (Prov. 18:21)*

Human words can hurt while God's Word heals. Who gets more credence will determine the state of your mental health. Measuring yourself against human standards is an emotional bouncy ball. One day you will feel up when you are well liked and down when you are in the disapproval rating. Ground yourself in God's opinion. When emotional wounds need salve, immediately choose to forgive the offender as Christ forgives you. Don't wait for your emotions to agree. Forgiveness is of the spirit and resentment lies in the sinful flesh. Be mindful, the soul needs daily bathing in Christ. This is what dying to self is about. The believer's spirit desires God's ways. However, in the heat of emotion you may fear you can't forgive. Don't fear, only depend. Jesus will provide you with His grace to forgive. It is unnatural for mankind to forgo a wrong, so keep relying upon Christ. This will ensure you are walking in His love. As you walk with Jesus, your emotional pain will be attended to. Jesus promises to bind up your broken heart so rest your wounds in His breast. In the process of healing, please keep your eyes on Jesus, not your symptoms. Symptom observance will create a victim mentality.

> *And be ye kind one to another, tenderhearted, forgiving one another, even as God for Christ's sake hath forgiven you. (Eph. 4:32)*

> *I am crucified with Christ: nevertheless, I live; yet not I, but Christ liveth in me: and*

the life which I now live in the flesh I live by the faith of the Son of God, who loved me, and gave himself for me. (Gal. 2:20)

He healeth the broken in heart, and bindeth up their wounds. (Ps. 147:3)

Remaining in God's love assures protection from the evil one and preserves you from the root of bitterness. You don't need to fall into the devil's snare of revenge or destroy your own soul when an attack upon your self-esteem is on. Grace is not fair. You were forgiven when you did not deserve it.

Let all bitterness, and wrath, and anger, and clamour, and evil speaking, be put away from you, with malice. (Eph. 4:31)

Follow peace with all men, and holiness, without which no man shall see the Lord: Looking diligently lest any man fail of the grace of God; lest any root of bitterness springing up trouble you, and thereby many be defiled. (Heb. 12:14-15)

And walk in love as Christ also hath loved us, and hath given himself for us an offering and a sacrifice to God for a sweetsmelling savour. (Eph. 5:2)

Pursue Peace. Be a Peacekeeper. You are Not the Peace Creator.

Allow the Lord to take care of the person who hurls harmful statements your way. This is not your territory or task. Pray for those who persecute you and the Lord will perform His part. What matters is the judge of the universe is on your side.

If peace is not possible, you have done your part. You are to pursue peace and be a peacekeeper. You can't keep peace that is not present. The outcome of your actions is based on whether the other person will participate. Invite only, for there is no imposing of this gift. Remember, you are not the peace creator; Jesus is.

> *Now the **Lord of peace himself give you peace** always by all means. The Lord be with you all. (2 Thess. 3:16) (Emphasis, mine)*
>
> *But I say unto you, Love your enemies, bless them that curse you, do good to them that hate you, and pray for them which despitefully use you, and persecute you; That ye may be the children of your Father which is in heaven. for he maketh his sun to rise on the evil and on the good, and sendeth rain on the just and the unjust. (Matt. 5:44-45)*

Reassurance Based on His Righteousness

Even when you sin and blow it, do not be afraid to approach your Father. This is when you need reassurance that **His righteousness** has not been removed. Your right standing before the Father is not based on your works or perfection but on Jesus Christ's redemption. The Lord will never quit accepting you, even when others or your own opinion of yourself differs from His. Drink again of His love and be cleansed; for His forgiveness is like a river of peace.

> *And when he is come, he will reprove the world of sin, and **of righteousness**, and of judgment. Of sin, because they believe not on me; **Of righteousness, because I go to my Father**, and ye see me no more. (Jn. 16:8-10) (Emphasis, mine)*

> *For thus saith the Lord, Behold, I will extend peace to her like a river, and the glory of the Gentiles like a flowing stream: then shall ye suck, ye shall be borne upon her sides, and be dandled upon her knees. As one whom his mother comforteth, so will I comfort you; and ye shall be comforted in Jerusalem. (Is. 66:12-13)*

Victims of Abuse Need to Know the Victory of Christ

If you are in harm's way, ask Christ Jesus for wisdom. His Holy Spirit will guide you carefully. Jesus leads with peace. If you are being physically or emotionally abused, this is an abomination upon God's holy temple, which is you. Martyrs for the sake of the Gospel are in a different class of people. A belief you deserve to be beaten up for any other reason is a form of self-righteousness. Jesus was the only one who was chosen to be beaten and spit upon for the sake of your sin. Your redemption for a guilty conscience has been paid for so you cannot add anything to His perfect work. Victims of abuse need to know the victory of Christ. If Christ is not the center of a belief system, twisted thinking occurs. The recording of lies need to be erased. Stop listening to the lies keeping you and other members of your family in cruelty. It is time to call out this sin occurring behind closed doors. Let us open them wide to the world and expose the devil. Also, you need not be ashamed of someone else's sin; it is not a reflection of who you are so shake off this bondage. God's truth will set you free.

> *Order my steps in thy word: and let not any iniquity have dominion over me. (Ps. 119:133)*

These things have I written unto you concerning them that seduce you. But the anointing which ye have received of him abideth in you, and ye need not that any man teach you: but as the same anointing teacheth you of all things, and is truth, and is no lie, and even as it hath taught you, ye shall abide in him. (1 Jn. 2:26-27)

For ye shall go out with joy and be led forth with peace: the mountains and the hills shall break forth before you into singing, and all the trees of the field shall clap their hands. (Is. 55:12)

And the work of righteousness shall be peace; and the effect of righteousness quietness and assurance forever. And my people shall dwell in a peaceable habitation, and in sure dwellings, and in quiet resting places. (Is. 32:17-18)

Love is Not Power and Control

Maybe confusion has captivated you. Do not allow anyone to misuse God's Word to keep you under domination. If you are uncertain of Biblical interpretation, study the Word. The Holy Spirit will enlighten you. The entire Scripture supports that love is neither power nor control. The Father who orchestrates the universe never misuses His power. Love protects and does not punish. Again, Jesus took your punishment, and no person can take your Savior's place. Discern between good and evil. Love, my beloved friend, is kind and doesn't think on evil.

> *Charity suffereth long, and is kind; charity envieth not; charity vaunteth not itself, is not puffed up, Doth not behave itself unseemly, seeketh not her own, is not easily provoked, thinketh no evil. (1 Cor.13:4-5)*

Don't Fear the Future

Finally, my fellow believer, do not fear the future. Your needs will be met and will overflow from Heaven's treasure house down to earth. The Father who creates cities and streets of gold will open His hand of provision. Ask Him and believe in His goodness. Nurture your faith in Christ Jesus by reading His Word and discovering His thoughts. They only possess peace, not evil. The Father says He will give you hope and a future. Step out in faith and follow the leading of the Holy Spirit. Fear not, your path is secure in your Savior.

> *But my God shall supply all your need according to his riches in glory by Christ Jesus. (Phil. 4:19)*

And the building of the wall of it was of jasper: and the city was pure gold, like unto clear glass. (Rev. 21:18)

And the twelve gates were twelve pearls; every several gate was of one pearl: and the street of the city was pure gold, as it were transparent glass. (Rev. 21:21)

He restoreth my soul: he leadeth me in paths of righteousness for his name's sake. (Ps. 23:3)

Ask and it shall be given you; seek, and ye shall find; knock, and it shall be opened unto you: For everyone that asketh receiveth; and he that seeketh findeth; and to him that knocketh it shall be opened. (Matt. 7:7-8)

For I know the thoughts that I think toward you, saith the Lord, thoughts of peace, and not of evil, to give you an expected end. (Jer. 29:11)

My people are destroyed for lack of knowledge. (Hosea 4:6)

Day 5

Cages Constructed With Lies

If you are living like a bird captive to its cage, seek the exit. Afraid to come out? Receive the strength to fly. Your wings are being clipped by fear. Fear constructs cages in the mind out of lies. The framework inhibits people from freely functioning. Afraid to leave their homes, fly in planes or be in crowds; the list of reasons people live without freedom is endless. Breaking out of the construction is not as complicated as you think. Simply ask your Savior to set you free.

> *But they that wait upon the Lord shall renew their strength; they shall mount up with wings as eagles; they shall run, and not be weary; and they shall walk, and not faint. (Is. 40:31)*

Meditate on Scripture

How will Jesus release you from your cage? By speaking to your soul through His written Word. It is within these holy pages you will receive answers for your problems and the strength to solve them. Peer into the sacred Scriptures and great and mighty things will unfold.

> *Call unto me, and I will answer thee, and shew thee great and mighty things, which thou knowest not. (Jer. 33:3)*

The wisdom you will receive is unlike the world's. You won't find fear's solution in self-help blogs or textbooks. As the eyes of your heart are enlightened to truth, you will look upon fear as folly. Satan has been fooling you to submit to his suggestions. He might even tell you to be afraid of him. The truth is, Satan is afraid of God and so also of you. Jesus Christ has demolished the devil's power and your cage is only a mirage. If the devil can distract you from the truth, his claws are able to sink lies into the depths of your mind. Decline his foolishness, you already possess power to fly.

> *For **the preaching of the cross** is to them that perish foolishness; but unto us which are saved it **is the power of God**. For it is written, I will destroy the wisdom of*

the wise, and will bring to nothing the understanding of the prudent. Where is the wise? Where is the scribe? Where is the disputer of this world? Hath not God made foolish the wisdom of this world? For after that in the wisdom of God the world by wisdom knew not God, it pleased God by the foolishness of preaching to save them that believe. (1 Cor. 1:18-21) (Emphasis, mine)

Because the foolishness of God is wiser than men, and the weakness of God is stronger than men. (1 Cor. 1:25)

The eyes of your understanding being enlightened, that ye may know what is the hope of his calling, and what the riches of the glory of his inheritance in the saints, And what is the exceeding greatness of his power to us-ward who believe, according to the working of his mighty power, Which he wrought in Christ, when he raised him from the dead, and set him at his own right hand in the heavenly places. Far above all principality, and power, and might, and dominion, and every name that is named, not only in this world, but also in that which is to come. And hath put all things

*under his feet and gave him to be the head
over all things to the church. (Eph.1:18-22)*

Are you ready to be released from your captivity? No cages can contain you when Jesus says you are free.

If the Son therefore shall make you free, ye shall be free indeed. (Jn. 8:36)

Day 6
Comfort is in a Covenant

We live in a comfort driven society. People shop the spectrum from recliners to clothes until their bodies find rest. Millions of people scurry up mall escalators and impatiently waltz through revolving doors. Consumers are chasing a sale before their hard-earned checks reach the bank. We layer our stress with style. Dressing rooms are filled with people trying to fit in; hoping a wardrobe can change their status. Behind these doors hang mirrors, bearing images of weary, fabricated lives.

Shopping has a way to drain both our energy and bank accounts. Advertisements flash hopeful diets while the diseased remain in hospital beds. The media and research continue to direct our choices. One day the food we used to enjoy is cast onto a blacklist for us to destroy. Grocery carts are only filling up with more confusion.

Wearing or reading labels may serve us satisfaction until the trend changes. Considering the climate of our society, I suggest it consider purchasing diving gear; for it is going to drown in the low tide of its values. If only people could see the price tag on their lives has more value than what is on racks and shelves. While they are busy working to spend money, Jesus gives the world this warning:

> *Labour not for the meat which perisheth, but for that meat which endureth unto everlasting life, which the Son of man shall give unto you: for him hath God the Father sealed. (Jn. 6:27)*

Jesus advises investment of energy into that which endures, not corrodes. He directs us to dine on fine foods which require no currency. May we say yes to His invitation.

> *Ho, every one that thirsteth, come ye to the waters, and he that hath no money; come ye, buy, and eat; yea, come, buy wine and milk without money and without price. Wherefore do ye spend money for that which is not bread? And your labour for that which satisfieth not? Hearken diligently unto me, and eat ye that which is good, and let your soul delight itself in fatness. Incline your ear, and come unto me: hear, and your soul shall live, and I will*

Comfort Is In A Covenant

> *make an everlasting covenant with you,*
> *even the sure mercies of David. (Is. 55:1-3)*

Jesus is calling His people to Himself. He is the wine, milk, and bread. The life he tells us to invest in contains a comfort we can't find in the world. Comfort in the Biblical sense means to call to one's side. When we draw near to Jesus, we hear Him calling us into an everlasting covenant. A covenant is a relationship between two parties who promise to work toward a common cause. In this covenant, unlike others in the Old Testament, the work is distinctly different. Entering the covenant with God is not based on human performance, but on believing in the one promised through David's lineage, Jesus. Today we live in the fulfillment of God's covenant through His finished work on the cross.

> *Then said they unto him, What shall we do, that we might work the works of God? Jesus answered and said unto them, This is the work of God, that ye believe on him whom he hath sent. (Jn. 6:28-29)*

Do you see the deal for a delightful life is sealed by trusting in our Savior? He has removed our label of sin and clothed us in righteousness. In the Father's world, it is all about relationship. There is no method or magic formula for us to follow. Dining with Jesus will discard our hurried, ragged lives. He soothes our worried minds, eliminating our need for comfort food on a depressing day. My fellow believer, the answer to our laboring lives is in our Lord Jesus Christ. Now take your concerns for food, health, and clothing to Jesus.

> *Take therefore no thought for the morrow: for the morrow shall take thought for the things of itself. Sufficient unto the day is the evil thereof. (Matt. 6:34)*

> *Behold, I will bring it health and cure, and I will cure them, and will reveal unto them the abundance of peace and truth. (Jer. 33:6)*

> *And why take ye thought for raiment? Consider the lilies of the field, how they grow; they toil not, neither do they spin. (Matt. 6:28)*

Jesus is concerned about your earthly existence. You certainly can be wise about taking care of yourself. However, don't forget, the next time a plateful of lies is serving anxiety, push it aside. Worry works against life. It will only add anti-aging creams to your shopping list. Be aware, this new worry-free attitude will create some discord.

Which of you by taking thought can add one cubit unto his stature? (Matt. 6:27)

There is a cost to following Jesus. When people realize you aren't sharing the menu of their anguish, they might cut you out of their social circles. Misery loves company. Is this worth your choice? While society may challenge your values, leave their confusion in the shopping cart. Your lifestyle will fashion the hope our world longs for. Bearing witness to a peace they cannot understand, will certainly be worth another soul's salvation. Remain faithful to the Father, this relationship is the one worth living for.

> *For which of you, intending to build a tower, sitteth not down first, and counteth the cost, whether he have sufficient to finish it? Lest haply, after he hath laid the foundation, and is not able to finish it, all that behold it begin to mock him. So likewise, whosoever he be of you that forsaketh not all that he hath, he cannot be my disciple. (Lk.14:28-29,33)*

> *And the peace of God, which passeth all understanding, shall keep your hearts and minds through Christ Jesus. (Phil. 4:7)*

But sanctify the Lord God in your hearts: and be ready always to give an answer to every man that asketh you a reason of the hope that is in you with meekness and fear. (1 Pet. 3:15)

Day 7
The Cup of Grief or Grace

Does your soul look more like a cracked cup seeping tears of sorrow rather than containing the joy of the Lord? If so, consider the cup of salvation.

> *I will take the cup of salvation, and call upon the name of the LORD. (Ps. 116:13)*

> *Then he said unto them, Go your way, eat the fat, and drink the sweet, and send portions unto them for whom nothing is prepared: for this day is holy unto our Lord: neither be ye sorry; for the joy of the Lord is your strength. (Neh. 8:10)*

If you choose the cup of grief, you will drink in its symptoms. A few examples are depression, hopelessness, insomnia, disease, confusion, and fear. Fear is a common factor in grief because losing anything stirs up insecurity. Spending time in sorrow causes decline in physical and mental health. King David provides a good description of his grief in the following passage.

> *For my life is spent with grief, and my years with sighing: my strength faileth because of my iniquity, and my bones are consumed. (Ps. 31:10)*

Grief pages back before David's time. If you read my book, *Leaving Grief at Heaven's Gate*, I describe how Adam and Eve's first connection with sorrow occurred when they ingested the fruit of rebellion. They immediately were separated from the Father who was their source of peace, love, and joy. Death was to be their destiny. The Father presented a plan of redemption, but they left the garden with sorrowing hearts.

We hear people cry as their personal paradise is swept away. My pen could create volumes of examples of loss. You can add your own grief to this short list: the death of a loved one, a divorce, declining health, a dream, loss of job or finances, imprisonment, and addiction. The ultimate grief is separation from the Heavenly Father. Oh, how glorious the cross is to remove us from this sorrow.

It was on the cross, Jesus Christ triumphed over sin, emptying the cup of its power. Only Jesus could drink in suffering, forgive our sin, and cancel its curse. The sacrifice was all done outside the gates of Heaven. Nothing sinful or unclean can enter the Holy of Holies.

The Cup Of Grief Or Grace

Once the payment for sin was paid, Jesus rose in righteousness, taking us with Him. Sitting with Him in Heavenly places does not mean we are sipping drinks of sorrow. Jesus left grief behind and so should you. He invites you to partake in His salvation rather remain in sadness. Jesus loves you too much to leave you with an empty cup. Why don't you let Him fill it up?

> *And hath raised us up together, and made us sit together in heavenly places in Christ Jesus. (Eph. 2:6)*
>
> *Thou preparest a table before me in the presence of mine enemies: thou anointest my head with oil; my cup runneth over. (Ps. 23:5)*

Day 8

Does Healing Really Happen Today?

Does healing really happen today? The topic of healing has built walls of conflict within our churches. We sit in confused pews when denominations differ in their interpretation of Scripture. While there are sincere but misguided ministers, there are also dangerous false prophets.

> *Add thou not unto his words, lest he reprove thee, and thou be found a liar. (Prov. 30:6)*

> *Now the Spirit speaketh expressly, that in the latter times some shall depart from the faith, giving heed to seducing spirits, and doctrines of devils; Speaking lies in hypocrisy; having their conscience seared with a hot iron. (1 Tim. 4:1-2)*

Who is right? While it is in God's order to have ministers to teach us, we also have a responsibility to study the Scriptures for ourselves.

> *Study to shew thyself approved unto God, a workman that needeth not to be ashamed, rightly dividing the word of truth. (2 Tim. 2:15)*

Check to see if what comes out of the pulpit is founded on the pure Word of God. Contaminated doctrine deceives the ignorant. You can safeguard yourself by asking for the wisdom to know God's will.

> *If any of you lack wisdom, let him ask of God, that giveth to all men liberally, and upbraideth not; and it shall be given him. (James 1:5)*

> *And this is the confidence that we have in him, that, if we ask anything according to his will, he heareth us: And if we know that he hear us, whatsoever we ask, we know that we have the petitions that we desired of him. (1 Jn. 5:14-15)*

Through the written Word, the Holy Spirit will answer your request by pointing you to Jesus. In Christ Jesus the wisdom you seek is revealed.

Howbeit, when he, the Spirit of truth, is come, he will guide you into all truth: for he shall not speak of himself; but whatsoever he shall hear, that shall he speak: and he will shew you things to come. He shall glorify me: for he shall receive of mine, and shall shew it unto you. All things that the Father hath are mine: therefore said I, that he shall take of mine, and shall shew it unto you. (Jn. 16:13-15)

That the God of our Lord Jesus Christ, the Father of glory, may give unto you the spirit of wisdom and revelation in the knowledge of him: The eyes of your understanding being enlightened; that ye may know what is the hope of his calling, and what the riches of the glory of his inheritance in the saints, And what is the exceeding greatness of his power to us-ward who believe, according to the working of his mighty power. (Eph. 1:17-19)

Now back to the question on healing. Let your heart ponder the work of Christ Jesus in the verse below. The cross reveals what riches are included in your inheritance. Read God's will or testament very carefully. Salvation is deliverance from sin and its consequences. Wouldn't this mean your soul, which includes the seat of feelings,

Does Healing Really Happen Today?

is delivered too? Many Christians have received the gift of forgiveness without question, but they reason their way out of physical healing.

> *Surely he hath borne our griefs, and carried our sorrows: yet we did esteem him stricken, smitten of God, and afflicted. But he was wounded for our transgressions, he was bruised for our iniquities. The chastisement of our peace was upon him; and with his stripes we are healed. (Is. 53:4-5)*

The term "griefs" really refers to sickness in the original language. "Stripes" refer to the wounds He endured when scourged. Since anxiety is a result of sin and is manifesting as an emotional illness, Jesus paid for it too. Every physical and emotional disease was atoned (forgiven). Scripture presents its case; the spirit, soul and body are to be made whole.

> *And the very God of peace sanctify you wholly; and I pray God your whole spirit and soul and body be preserved blameless unto the coming of our Lord Jesus Christ. Faithful is he that calleth you, who also will do it. (1 Thess. 5:23-24)*

As you study this subject for yourself, be sure to let scripture interpret scripture to gain an accurate understanding. There is no denying the entire Bible holds numerous accounts of healing. From the Old to New Testament, healing has happened. For example, under the Old Testament covenant, a leper followed atoning sacrifices to receive healing. (See Lev.14:1-32) Every sacrifice in the Old Testament pointed to the crucifixion of Jesus Christ. The New Testament requires no animal blood; for Jesus Christ came to shed His own blood on our behalf. He was the fulfillment of the Old Testament rituals. Also, if it wasn't the Father's will to heal, why would Jesus perform these miraculous wonders while He walked on earth? He surely revealed the Father's heart of compassion. We must not miss another point of interest; Jesus refused not one person who needed help.

> *So Jesus had compassion on them, and touched their eyes: and immediately their eyes received sight, and they followed him. (Matt. 20:34)*

> *And he touched her hand, and the fever left her: and she arose, and ministered unto them. (Matt. 8:15)*

> *Then they went out to see what was done; and came to Jesus, and found the man, out of whom the devils were departed, sitting*

at the feet of Jesus, clothed, and in his right mind: and they were afraid. (Lk. 8:35)

That was then, but what about today? Jesus left clear instructions to carry on His work after He departed. Wow, that is quite an undertaking, or is it? Jesus doesn't expect us to save the lost, heal the sick or cast out demons with our own power. He knows we cannot. Therefore, the Holy Spirit equips us with the power to perform such extraordinary deeds. Don't worry, it is God's Word that does the work. We do the speaking. The Gospel message has brought multitudes of people their desired healing.

> *And as ye go, preach, saying, The kingdom of heaven is at hand. Heal the sick, cleanse the lepers, raise the dead, cast out devils: freely ye have received, freely give. (Matt. 10:7-8)*
>
> *And I will pray the Father, and he shall give you another Comforter, that he may abide with you forever. (Jn. 14:16)*

Discern for yourself. Doctrines can differ and change with interpretation, but Jesus does not. Will you put more credence in theological debates, a diagnosis or what Jesus demonstrates? It was with great suffering He overcame anxiety. We are back to the beginning.

Answer the question after consideration of God's Word, ***Does Healing Really Happen Today?***

> *Jesus Christ the same yesterday, and to day, and for ever. (Heb. 13:8)*

> *These things I have spoken unto you, that in me ye might have peace. In the world ye shall have tribulation: but be of good cheer; I have overcome the world. (Jn. 16:33)*

Day 9
Treating Symptoms Without the Savior

Professionals are developing treatment plans for their clients which are research based. A common modality is Cognitive Behavioral Therapy. This tool replaces lies with truthful statements. There are numerous methods such as relaxation techniques or exposure therapy which offer benefit in symptom management. However, these skills cannot help clients leap the fence to freedom.

Secular therapy believes it can put a bridle on the sinful flesh. Their methods will only give the flesh more gumption to rebel. Why? The carnal nature is like a bucking bronco. It becomes defiant when commanding reins insist control. Working within the context of our own nature fails miserably. The more we try the more frustrated we become because we draw strength from our own reserve. Scripture states sin is brought to life when presented with the law. We cannot live up to perfection apart from Christ Jesus. Mental health treatment is frankly inadequate for full transformation of the mind. Therefore, submission to a sensible and orderly life requires a spiritual revolution.

> *But sin, taking occasion by the commandment, wrought in me all manner of concupiscence. For without the law sin was dead. (Rom. 7:8)*

It is time to bring reformation into the realm of counseling. Therapy has reversed God's order for operating. The secular world looks horizontally, not vertically for help. Within the horizon we have a big picture of SELF, not our Savior. For instance, many clients using Cognitive Behavioral Therapy do not depend on Jesus Christ as their basis for truth. Truth becomes relative. Humanism cannot help suffering people. There are innate needs secular counseling cannot and never will meet. Human beings need tending in their spirits before their minds and bodies will manifest change. Christians, let us stand with open Bibles and offer the true plans of liberty.

> *The Spirit of the Lord is upon me, because he hath anointed me to preach the gospel to the poor; he hath sent me to heal the broken-hearted, to preach deliverance to the captives, and recovering of sight to the blind, to set at liberty them that are bruised,*

*To preach the acceptable year of the Lord.
(Lk. 4:18-19)*

Christian and pastoral counselors recognize the carnal mind needs Christ Jesus. Whether the mind is regenerate or not, determines the appropriate course of action. Unsaved souls need introduction to the God who will forgive their sins and heal their condition. Believers need encouragement in their walk with their Savior.

The virtue of Christ Jesus brings temperance by relinquishing strongholds in the mind. It is the whisper of love which tames hearts. The whip of judgment has been put down by the forgiving hand of Christ Jesus. Bondage to fear has been set free from its stall. Beautiful is the soul who has been released from the binding reins of sin.

My heart pleads to the counseling world. Pull another chair into your office. Invite Jesus to take the chair of authority. Erase your discouraging treatment plans and put the Word of God into place. Witness the Holy Spirit harnessing the enemy and hushing its voice of harassment. Disorders transform into order as the sinful nature relinquishes its power. A mind filled with peace is the result. Is this not the goal for every treatment plan? It all begins with God.

> *For they that are after the flesh do mind the things of the flesh; but they that are after the Spirit the things of the Spirit.*

*For to be carnally minded is death; but to be spiritually minded is life and peace. Because the carnal mind is enmity against God: for it is not subject to the law of God, neither indeed can be. So then they that are in the flesh cannot please God. But ye are not in the flesh, but in the Spirit, if so be that the Spirit of God dwell in you. Now if any man have not the Spirit of Christ, he is none of his. And if Christ be in you, the body is dead because of sin; but the Spirit is life because of righteousness. But if the Spirit of him that raised up Jesus from the dead dwell in you, he that raised up Christ from the dead shall also quicken your mortal bodies by his Spirit that dwelleth in you. Therefore, brethren, we are not debtors, not to the flesh, to live after the flesh. For if ye live after the flesh, ye shall die: but if ye through the Spirit do mortify the deeds of the body, ye shall live. For as many as are led by the Spirit of God, they are the sons of God. For ye have **not received the spirit of bondage again to fear**, but ye have received the Spirit of adoption, whereby we cry, Abba, Father. The Spirit itself beareth witness with our spirit, that we are the children of God: And if children, then heirs, heirs of God, and joint-heirs with Christ; if* *so be that we suffer with him that we may be also glorified together. (Romans 8:5-17) (Emphasis mine)*

Day 10
Get Off the Hamster Wheel

Living with anxiety is likened to running on a hamster wheel. Daily exercise with fear will create a regimented routine, giving it strength while offering no rest. Overdoing it can lead to a mental and physical breakdown. Trying to hop off the wheel and dash away won't work. The escape plan fails because fear chases its victim back on. Examine the engineering of the wheel. It is crafted with tools of falsehood. Who is responsible for such design is the devil. The devil knows his wheel has great force when propelled by lies. So, the devil throws deceitful thoughts out like breadcrumbs. Enticing thoughts are like bait and if eaten can be very believable. Collecting deceitful thoughts with each turn generates more fuel. As the wheel turns it makes one's head to spin. It is constantly rotating confusion.

> *Ye are of your father the devil, and the lusts of your father ye will do. He was a*

murderer from the beginning, and abode not in the truth, because there is no truth in him. When he speaketh a lie, he speaketh of his own: for he is a liar, and the father of it. (Jn. 8:44)

Mixing fear into truth can make it harder to discern reality. People take the lies to heart and believe their fearful state of mind is the basis of truth. They begin living out their fears through their imagination. It is a trick of the devil to bring a believer's belief system out from the Holy of Holies down into the pit of hellish thinking. It takes more than psychotherapy to change minds. Clients need Christ Jesus. His obedient work on the cross is far more powerful than a college filled with professors teaching Cognitive Behavioral Therapy.

Casting down imaginations, and every high thing that exalteth itself against the knowledge of God, and bringing into captivity every thought to the obedience of Christ. (2 Cor. 10:5)

I have mentioned Cognitive Behavioral Therapy (CBT) in a previous writing. CBT is a tool helping clients to replace thoughts filled with lies with truth. Behaviors will change when belief systems are recreated via one thought at a time. It bears repeating; this all sounds innocent and trustworthy to the average person.

However, these mental exercises or any type of mindfulness present concerns. First, if the client's foundation of truth is not Christ Jesus, we have humanism. Secondly, mental gymnastics are trying to compete against a spiritual enemy. Secular mental health practitioners and their clients don't possess the power in their vocabulary to set anyone free. Anxiety will only be annulled by God's truth.

> *For the word of God is quick, and powerful, and sharper than any twoedged sword, piercing even to the dividing asunder of soul and spirit, and of the joints and marrow, and is a discerner of the thoughts and intents of the heart. (Heb. 4:12)*

> *And ye shall know the truth, and the truth shall make you free. (Jn. 8:32)*

Rational based assignments promote self-effort and disqualify our Savior. A client is asked to be their own god. They are led to believe the power of right thinking can break the cycle of fear or any emotional distress. See the sly maneuver of the serpent? Not only do clients have fearful imaginations, but secular counseling compiles it with the notion that fear is disposed of through the power in oneself. Fear, secular therapy, and the god of self will keep the wheel in motion. Will you believe it only takes the true Word to dismantle this operation?

> *He that committeth sin is of the devil; for the devil sinneth from the beginning. For this purpose the Son of God was manifested, that he might destroy the works of the devil. (1 Jn. 3:8)*

Your mind doesn't have to be left spinning. Jesus Christ will stop the wheel and any other weapon coming against you with His Word! Ready to get off?

> *No weapon that is formed against thee shall prosper; and every tongue that shall rise against thee in judgment thou shalt condemn. This is the heritage of the servants of the LORD, and their righteousness is of me, saith the LORD. (Is. 54:17)*

Day 11

What About Will Power?

How many books or websites are you willing to read pertaining to health? Whether it is physical or mental health you are aiming to improve, the research appears to be running on a trendy treadmill. Studies quickly shift their speed before you can digest your last meal. The focus on fitness has become obsessively discouraging. Failing to bring harmony into the body and mind, society prods on with catchy innovations. Science cleverly changes its course while pumping up your willpower. You become hooked with false hope. Determined to diet and exercise or ditch your diagnosis and addiction, the destiny is to feel better. Unfortunately, the treadmill of trends has one revolving track. Never moving forward, yet you are driven to run with its promising programs. Knowledge races into your mind as motivational speakers inject you with attractive adrenaline. Purchasing manuals which mask the truth, you innocently buy into their jargon. Human intelligence never stops building a Tower of Babel. Each brick burdens you with more pride. Striving to reach the stars of success, you stumble over yourself. The new language still speaks about the old theme of will power. Its trends took you right back to the beginning where you are left to empower yourself. Discouragement causes you to trip and fall off your regime. Humbly you admit, your **will** holds no enduring **power** to achieve. Research has only scattered your mind even more. You are perplexed when the plan does not promote God. Silence this babble and stop sitting in classrooms scorning true wisdom.

> *Blessed is the man that walketh not in the counsel of the ungodly, nor standeth in the way of sinners, nor sitteth in the seat of the scornful. (Ps. 1:1)*

Confusion comes when conforming to the world. Therefore, separate yourself from these shenanigans and devote your mind to Christ. When the will of God is translated into your heart, the power to succeed prevails. With God's will and power in place, the Spirit stirs delightful desires into your soul.

> *And be not conformed to this world: but be ye transformed by the renewing of your mind, that ye may prove what is that good, and acceptable, and perfect, will of God. (Rom.12:2)*

But we have the mind of Christ. (1 Cor. 2:16)

I delight to do thy will, O my God: yea, thy law is within my heart. (Ps. 40:8)

Brilliant Scriptures will pinnacle over people's power points. When you hunger for His Holiness, the Word of truth steps over corruption and guides you back to the cross. A fresh commitment to health begins at Calvary. Spend considerable time here before you miss the mystery unfold.

But we speak the wisdom of God in a mystery, even the hidden wisdom, which God ordained before the world unto our glory: Which none of the princes of this world knew: for had they known it, they would not have crucified the Lord of glory. (1 Cor. 2:7-8)

As you study the cross, the Spirit sweeps you out of bondage. No longer will you depend upon deception when deliverance comes into view. Christ's beaming light reveals it is the Father's will for your body and soul to prosper.

Beloved, I wish above all things that thou mayest prosper and be in health, even as thy soul prospereth. (3 Jn. 1:2)

Dullened senses arouse as your heart views the beaten body of Jesus, stricken with every sickness for your sake. You hear the announcement from the inner court, the payment for sin, sickness, disease, and all poverty known to mankind has been paid.

I pray you believe in the mystery hidden from the world. Can you see your precious Savior presenting you with a gift card filled with health? Love directed His purchase, oh so long ago. He sees your name carefully written and sealed in the Book of Life. Life is in this Book my friend, not pages scribbled with your diagnosis and disease. Dare not deny the sacrifice providing you with divine prosperity. Jesus awaits. What you believe won't change His holy offer.

Who his own self bare our sins in his own body on the tree, that we, being dead to sins, should live unto righteousness: by whose stripes ye were healed. (1 Pet. 2:24)

For what if some did not believe? shall their unbelief make the faith of God without effect? (Rom. 3:3)

All because of the cross, health springs into your mind and body. It takes a healthy body to possess the power to keep fit! Now quickly hasten to peer at the Holy Spirit's power raising Jesus and you to the Father's side. Healing wings have gently placed you into heaven's position.

If ye then be risen with Christ, seek those things which are above, where Christ sitteth on the right hand of God. (Col. 3:1)

But unto you who fear my name shall the Sun of righteousness arise with healing in his wings; and ye shall go forth, and grow up as calves of the stall. (Mal. 4:2)

New strength surges as the Spirit joins you in performing God's perfect will. Taking care of your temple is on the list. The Holy Spirit will impart to you wisdom and power to maintain a healthy lifestyle. You are made by a marvelous Creator, so please trust Him as your trainer. Jesus Christ will not only give you knowledge, but His authority as well.

What About Will Power?

What? know ye not that your body is the temple of the Holy Ghost which is in you, which ye have of God, and ye are not your own? For ye are bought with a price: therefore glorify God in your body, and in your spirit, which are God's. (1 Cor. 6:19-20)

Now we have received, not the spirit of the world, but the spirit which is of God; that we might know the things that are freely given to us of God. (1 Cor. 2:12)

I will praise thee; for I am fearfully and wonderfully made: marvellous are thy works; and that my soul knoweth right well. (Ps. 139:14)

Maybe you aren't aware of the authority you share. There is a reason you are spiritually sitting at the Father's right hand with Jesus. You possess the keys to the kingdom governing over the lust of your flesh and every failure to thrive. Operating with this privilege requires a position of reliance. Stay humbly seated for your good intentions and human knowledge hold no merit here. It is the Spirit who flushes out the fleshly customs fancying your faith. Never dismiss the divine; the nails binding all sinful habits have been broken with resurrection power. Jesus Christ frees you to a lifestyle filled with fitness and health. His righteousness replaces the rudiments of the laws you have been following.

> *And I will give unto thee the keys of the kingdom of heaven: and whatsoever thou shalt bind on earth shall be bound in heaven: and whatsoever thou shalt loose on earth shall be loosed in heaven. (Matt. 16:19)*

> *For this I say then, Walk in the Spirit, and ye shall not fulfil the lust of the flesh. (Gal. 5:16)*

> *Beware lest any man spoil you through philosophy and vain deceit, after the tradition of men, after the rudiments of the world, and not after Christ. (Col. 2:8)*

Standing at the foot of the cross shatters earthly mirrors. Reliance upon the world's ways or your own self, holds no attraction. Worship, admiration, and adoration are reserved for your Savior. As your image fades into His, resurrected power emerges. You are not stuck in a routine with will power but are lifted onto the right track of life.

> *Jesus said unto her, I am the resurrection, and the life: he that believeth in me, though he were dead, yet shall he live. (Jn. 11:25)*

I am crucified with Christ: nevertheless I live; yet not I, but Christ liveth in me: and the life which I now live in the flesh I live by the faith of the Son of God, who loved me, and gave himself for me. (Gal. 2:20)

Day 12
Two Choices

Life in a culture of choices can be confounding. When we dine at a new restaurant we read the menu, pour over the reviews, examine passing entrees, drill the server, check the prices, count the calories, and doubt our decision until the food arrives. We wait in unease and hope the dish measures up to its cost. The event generates more complications than cooking at home. However, if you frequent your favorite place, your mind is made up before you enter the door. Your palate knows what plate to choose. It simply makes for an effortless and enjoyable time. Many would agree, this is no different when finding healthcare. May this message assist you with the menu of options. It won't be complicated when you realize there are only two choices. The decision will determine if your experience will be difficult or divine. It all depends on which tree you choose to eat from.

Two Trees
First Choice: The Tree of Life.

The Father throws you an exquisite feast, unlike any other. An invitation is sent with hands scarred by your sin. The gates of His Kingdom swing open as you behold the Tree of Life. Uncertain the tree is true; bells of impossibility deafen His call to dine. Hear Him while the door remains open. Despise not His Word. Shun the scoffers who spit on your Savior's supper. They thwart your way to liberty. For the table of grace frees this fearful heart of yours. The Lord of Hosts has prepared for this day. While flaming angels were sent to guard Eden's gates, the Tree of Life chose to die on the cross. The veil between Heaven and earth is removed. This is your first choice my friend. Shall I provide an explanation why a tree can offer life?

Explanation:

Who is this Tree of Life? Scripture interpreting Scripture reveals the tree to be Jesus Christ. Jesus is portrayed as the true vine and we as the branches. This vineyard is attended to by our Father. In the vineyard is your body and soul. The Father is busy removing unbelieving branches which hinder His fruits from growing. To increase the production of fruit, He cleanses our branches as we soak in His Word. What value there is in reading Holy Scriptures.

> *I am the true vine, and my Father is the husbandman. Every branch in me that beareth not fruit he taketh away: and every branch that beareth fruit, he purgeth it, that it may bring forth more fruit. (Jn. 15:1-2)*

> *That he might sanctify and cleanse it with the washing of water by the word. (Eph. 5:26)*

What has the Tree of Life done for us? The Tree of Life has fulfilled the requirements of the law. To live in the presence of perfection, sin must be removed. Religious rules are replaced with a relationship with the Father.

> *Having abolished in his flesh the enmity, even the law of commandments contained in ordinances; for to make in himself of twain one new man, so making peace;*

> *And that he might reconcile both unto God in one body by the cross, having slain the enmity thereby. (Eph. 2:15-16)*

The law was given because God's people believed they were good enough without Him. The Father used the law to call His children back to His side. He wanted them to know the standard of perfect love couldn't be attained through their performance. There was another plan in place to help them. His Son was the promise to return them to Paradise. There are still those who choose to live by the law, thus believing their works deserve heavenly rewards. It is a dangerous road they travel. When legalism pushes God into the backseat, who is driving? May we preach the grace of God to the blind. Only Jesus Christ leads the way into the Kingdom of God.

> *But their minds were blinded. For until this day remaineth the same vail untaken away in the reading of the old testament; which vail is done away in Christ. But even unto this day, when Moses is read, the vail is upon their heart. Nevertheless, when it shall turn to the Lord, the vail shall be taken away. Now the Lord is that Spirit: and where the Spirit of the Lord is, there is liberty. But we all, with open face beholding as in a glass the glory of the Lord, are changed into the same image from glory to glory, even as by the Spirit of the Lord. (2 Cor. 3:14-18)*

The Tree of Life has opened the borders to God's Kingdom. The wall has fallen! The vail once separating sinners from the Holy of Holies is removed. Strangers and aliens become citizens, sharing rights with Jesus Christ.

> *But now in Christ Jesus ye who sometimes were far off are made nigh by the blood of Christ. (Eph. 2:13)*
>
> *And came and preached peace to you which were afar off, and to them that were nigh.*
>
> *For through him we both have access by one Spirit unto the Father. Now therefore ye are no more strangers and foreigners, but fellow citizens with the saints, and of the household of God. (Eph. 2:17-19)*

Finally, the Tree of Life is your healthcare. Jesus gives health and strength to your mind and body. He encompasses your every need. When you trust in Christ Jesus, the conduit for endless supply is unclogged. Heaven's gate swings open to shower you with blessings. Satisfying fruit supersedes the culmination of knowledge you have digested. No arduous studies or work is required, for fruit doesn't work at being fruit. God's prosperity is promised when branches remain connected to the vine.

> *In the midst of the street of it, and on either side of the river, was there the tree of life, which bare twelve manner of fruits, and yielded her fruit every month: and the*

leaves of the tree were for the healing of the nations. (Rev. 22:2)

But the fruit of the Spirit is love, joy, peace, longsuffering, gentleness, goodness, faith, Meekness, temperance: against such there is no law. (Gal. 5:22-23)

And he shall be like a tree planted by the rivers of water, that bringeth forth his fruit in his season; his leaf also shall not wither; and whatsoever he doeth shall prosper. (Ps. 1:3)

But my God shall supply all your need according to his riches in glory by Christ Jesus. (Phil. 4:19)

After gazing at the Tree of Life, do we really need to look at your other option? I began with God's selection since He doesn't want you to settle for second best. However, to honor your free will, may we continue to read the menu. Your second choice is the Tree of Knowledge of Good and Evil.

Second Choice: Tree of Knowledge of Good and Evil

The Tree of Knowledge of Good and Evil had a different purpose. Its fruit was not to be on Adam and Eve's menu. There has been much contention surrounding this tree. Challenging questions arise when someone's disobedience affects us all. I often hear believers complain about the Father's garden plans. They are mad He planted this tree into Eden. Blaming the Father doesn't make sense. Perhaps they don't know Him very well. Our Heavenly Father is a complete gentleman. His character is mannerly and lovely, never imposing or forcing His ways upon us. Imagine living under a dictator who doesn't respect our choices. Dreadful is the day our freedom of choice is stripped away. In the eyes of our wise Creator, the Tree of Knowledge of Good and Evil allowed Adam and Eve to exercise their gift of free will. Therefore, the tree was good like all of God's creation. The problem was not the tree but the people who ate from it.

> *And God saw every thing that he had made, and, behold, it was very good. (Gen. 1:31)*

Pride handcuffs us to problems. Believing we know better than God holds great consequences. The decision to eat the forbidden fruit changed the garden's praises into groans. The cries are heard today as sin continues to cause death and separation from the Father. The sadness started when a serpent seized an opportunity to twist God's truth. Curses still come when God's Word is tampered with. May we take Him seriously when He advises us to avoid ungodly counsel.

> *For I testify unto every man that heareth the words of the prophecy of this book, If any man shall add unto these things, God shall add unto him the plagues that are written in this book: And if any man shall take away from the words of the book of this prophecy, God shall take away his part out of the book of life, and out of the holy city, and from the things which are written in this book. (Rev. 22:18-19)*

Take heed, listening to erroneous advice can lead anyone astray. Eve's downfall began when she spent time with the wrong company, opening her mind to deception.

> *And the serpent said unto the woman, Ye shall not surely die: For God doth know that in the day ye eat thereof, then your eyes shall be opened, and ye shall be as gods, knowing good and evil. (Gen. 3:4-5)*

Before we gloat in our goodness stating we would never forsake God and ruin creation, examine our ways. When our Father says He will heal, provide, protect, and love us forever; do we believe? Our actions will prove the fruit in our hearts. If we are so pious, we wouldn't be medicating our minds, trusting the stock market, displaying our trophies, dancing with degrees, pounding our chests at games, hiding under covers, or giving credit to the cash for our provision. How easy to slip off the right path and act as gods. Beloved, seek God's wisdom to guide your ways.

Now that you viewed your menu's options, it is up to you. Will you choose to eat from the Tree of Life or the Tree of Knowledge of Good and Evil? The fruit differentiates between a divine or difficult experience. It is time, I hear the supper bell ringing.

> *Happy is the man that findeth wisdom, and the man that getteth understanding. (Prov. 3:13)*
>
> *Her ways are ways of pleasantness, and all her paths are peace. She is a tree of life to them that lay hold upon her: and happy is every one that retaineth her. (Prov 3: 17-18)*
>
> *The fruit of the righteous is a tree of life. (Prov. 11:30)*

And he saith unto me, Write, Blessed are they which are called unto the marriage supper of the Lamb. And he saith unto me, These are the true sayings of God. (Rev. 19:9)

Day 13
The Changing World

Casting God out of our government folds the flag of freedom. Losing our God-given rights is frightening. This should not spring surprise, for Scripture gives us warning. We not only study prophesy but are watching the predicted changes unfold.

> *And he shall speak great words against the most High, and shall wear out the saints of the most High, and think to change times and laws: and they shall be given into his hand until a time and times and the dividing of time. (Dan. 7:25)*

Ejecting Jesus Christ from our land effects our lives on many levels. Hope for prosperity pines away. During this perilous season we can either become depressed or depend upon Jesus. Wouldn't we rather side with the one providing us with peace? Jesus saved us from the enslavement of such stress. When our country's security loosens its stakes, recognize the real enemy lurking behind its officials. The oppression stems from powers of spiritual wickedness.

> *For we wrestle not against flesh and blood, but against principalities, against powers, against the rulers of the darkness of this world, against spiritual wickedness in high places. (Eph. 6:12)*

Jesus foresaw the evil forces we would encounter and warned us not to be troubled. He would equip us for the wrestle and make sure we wouldn't be pinned in the match. However, we need to listen to the Spirit's instruction for each move against our opponents. When the opposer becomes our own government, we have no time to play games. We have learned from history; God's people have been penciled into the devil's plan for destruction. As fear mongering troops maneuver before us, Jesus ushers in assistance for our tenuous souls. Be encouraged, threatening times do not have to create turbulent hearts.

> *And when ye shall hear of wars and rumours of wars, be ye not troubled: for such things must needs be; but the end shall not be yet. (Mk. 13:7)*

A Little but Loaded Word

One verse can reverse the enemy's hold on our lives. Read the passage below carefully. Jesus begins His statement with this little but loaded word, *let*. *Let* means we control the stop and go light. Will the light flash green or red when trouble drives up to our hearts? Tumultuous times have no right entering, but they can be extremely tantalizing. Keeping trouble out is only possible when we let God in. Sounds simple until someone snags us into negativity.

> *Let not your heart be troubled: ye believe in God, believe also in me. (Jn.14:1)*

Problems will always be busy painting dreadful pictures before our minds. The media splatters its political agenda, hoping to glue our attention to false gods. If our hearts feel like they're sinking, negativity succeeded in pulling us into its net. Instead of screen time, may we tune into the Good News. Our hearts will arise with hope as we recognize we are not lying on mats of defeat. Ultimately, Christ Jesus shoulders all government. May we never stop singing praises to whom our true allegiance lies.

> *And having spoiled principalities and powers, he made a shew of them openly, triumphing over them in it. (Col. 2:15)*

For unto us is born, unto us a son is given: and the government shall be upon his shoulder: and his name shall be called Wonderful, Counsellor, The mighty God, The everlasting Father, The Prince of Peace. Of the increase of his government and peace there shall be no end, upon the throne of David, and upon his kingdom, to order it, and to establish it with judgment and with justice from henceforth even for ever. The zeal of the LORD of hosts will perform this. (Is. 9: 6-7)

Invisible and Undefeatable

Have you given much thought to the role Jesus has in government? We just read Isaiah's prophesy and see authority belongs to Christ Jesus. Our Lord may be invisible, but He is undefeatable. The enemy knows his limitations and that his end of influence draws nigh. We don't have to let the devil scare us with ungodly force. We can call on Jesus. At the sound of His voice demons join pigs for a dive into the sea!

And, behold, they cried out, saying, What have we to do with thee, Jesus, thou Son of God? art thou come hither to torment us before the time? (Matt. 8:29)

And he said unto them, Go. And when they were come out, they went into the herd of swine: and, behold, the whole herd of swine ran violently down a steep place into the sea, and perished in the waters. (Matt. 8:32)

Speaking of the sea, tour back with me into the wilderness. There is an exodus which will bring us fresh encouragement. Why wait to watch the Ten Commandments when we have the story right before us. Go ahead and open your Bible to Exodus 15 chapter eight verses 8-11. Really take time to meditate on these miracles. We see Israelites treading through waters without wetness! Howling winds are blowing waters into walls of protection! The Lord drowns Pharoah's chariots who race after God's people! All the while, hidden in a cloud, Christ commands His people to trust Him over the troubling sights. Shall we remember this when our passage is perilous and scepters flash ungodly change into our lives? Let not our hearts be troubled but worship Him who performs wonders in the sea.

And with the blast of thy nostrils the waters were gathered together, the floods stood upright as an heap, and the depths were congealed in the heart of the sea. The enemy said, I will pursue, I will overtake, I will divide the spoil; my lust shall be satisfied upon them; I will draw my sword, my hand shall destroy them. Thou didst blow with thy wind, the sea covered them: they sank as lead in the mighty waters. Who is like unto thee, O LORD, among the gods? Who is like thee, glorious in holiness, fearful in praises, doing wonders? (Ex. 15: 8–11)

Day 14
Is Worry Worth a Badge?

We all have encountered people who brag about being a worrier. They pair their worry with a warrior who is skillful in caring. Before displaying this fretful badge as if it adds dignity to one's character, let's clear up any misconception. Worry is devised by the devil. He is hoping to develop his den in your home. Worry (what I refer to as anxiety or fear in a persistent state) robs you from the presence of Christ Jesus in your life. Where is God's peace when the mind is rolling in fearfulness? Fear is the weapon shooting you with lies. The devil's victory is acquired when you pay attention to him rather than God. Therefore, dismiss the temptation to focus on your problems. If the devil succeeds in building a den in your mind, distress will create various types of impairment.

> *Behold, ye trust in lying words, that cannot profit. (Jer. 7:8)*

And come and stand before me in this house, which is called by my name, and say, We are delivered to do all these abominations? (Jer. 7:10)

Physical problems such as panic attacks, heart failure, intestinal disorders, eczema, insomnia, or headaches are just a few examples resulting from anxiety. Some people turn to food, alcohol, drugs, gambling, or pornography to self-medicate their feelings. Try deadening fear by feeding your flesh and you will find yourself rolling in a negative snowball. Anxiety drives people away from social situations and affects their work and relationships. It drains energy, interferes with concentration and healthy exercise. So, is your worry worth a badge? Not at all. Fear needs to be stripped of its badge and kept out of sight. Rid this robber from your life by receiving God's grace. Salvation bundles in the deal of abundant peace. This is no ordinary peace and is foreign to intelligent studies. When depressed in your current state, humbly seek God's ways and delight in His gifts.

The thief cometh not, but for to steal, and to kill, and to destroy. I am come that thy might have life, and that they might have it more abundantly. (Jn. 10:10)

But the meek shall inherit the earth; and shall delight themselves in the abundance of peace. (Ps. 37:11)

Scholars wouldn't be scrutinizing the epidemic of anxiety if they took heed of God's Word. In the world of science, this solution appears too simplistic. Receiving power to free our minds from anxiety without some clinical intervention seems foolish. The unsaved can only grasp what makes sense to the carnal mind. The natural mind rejects Christ; therefore, their solutions are void of truth. Hushing the message of the cross prevents people from receiving Christ's amazing freedom.

For to be carnally minded is death, but to be spiritually minded is life and peace. Because the carnal mind is enmity against God: for it is not subject to the law of God, neither indeed can be. (Rom. 8:6-7)

For the preaching of the cross is to them that perish foolishness; but unto us which are saved it is the power of God. (1 Cor. 1:18)

But ye are not in the flesh, but in the Spirit, if so be that the Spirit of God dwell in you. Now if any man have not the Spirit of Christ, he is none of his. (Rom. 8:9)

Is Worry Worth A Badge?

Attempting to change our cognition on our terms, only opens the portal to hell. Lies spew out of deceiving pits and Christians need to put a lid on them. Don't tamper with the devil's territory and fall into despair. Disregarding God's truth gives fear the privilege to wander into our minds. Hang tight to the Word of Christ and remain free from spoiling your life with disgusting deceit. Nobody likes to be lied to. They destroy individuals, relationships, businesses, governments, and nations. Granting a single lie permission to rent space in the mind is like inviting a thief to sleep over. People slip under the covers with falsehood believing it to be their only option. The struggle becomes overwhelming to the point they give up and stay down. How senseless when Christ crucified fear over 2000 years ago and lifted us to victory. Get to know the truth rather than putting up with a defeated devil.

> *And cast him into the bottomless pit, and shut him up, and set a seal upon him, that he should deceive the nations no more, till the thousand years should be fulfilled: and after that he must be loosed a little season. (Rev. 20:3)*

> *And ye shall know the truth, and the truth shall make you free. (Jn. 8:32)*

No reason to stall, throw your badge of worry back into the pit. Find your delight in the truth and never open the lid of lies again.

> *Peace I leave with you, my peace I give unto you: not as the world giveth, give I unto you. Let not your heart be troubled, neither let it be afraid. (Jn. 14:27)*

Day 15

Angels

Yesterday we saw mighty seas crashing over chariots. Today we behold heavenly winds carrying warring chariots driven by angels. While we are not to worship these unseen warriors, we can appreciate their presence and understand what prompts their mission. The secret to their service is connected to God's Word.

> *The chariots of God are twenty thousand, even thousands of angels: the Lord is among them, as in Sinai, in the holy place. (Ps. 68:17)*

> *And I John saw these things, and heard them. And when I had heard and seen, I fell down to worship before the feet of the angel which shewed me these things. Then saith he unto me, See thou do it not: for I am thy fellowservant, and of thy brethren the prophets, and of them which*

keep the sayings of this book: worship God. (Rev. 22:8-9)

Heavenly beings are here to protect us from our visible and invisible enemies. They are ready to work when they hear the voice of God. Speaking God's Word sends them into operation. When fear pursues us like an angry bear, we can stop screaming and speak promises of protection instead. Fear can't penetrate the shield of truth. The enemy will meet defending angels and bump into the wings of the Almighty. Safely tucked under His shadow, we speak praises only to Him.

> *Bless the LORD, ye his angels, that excel in strength, that do his commandments, hearkening unto the voice of his word. Bless ye the LORD, all ye his hosts; ye ministers of his, that do his pleasure. (Ps. 103:20-21)*
>
> *He that dwelleth in the secret place of the most High shall abide under the shadow of the Almighty. (Ps. 91:1)*
>
> *He shall cover thee with his feathers, and under his wings shalt thou trust: his truth shall be thy shield and buckler. (Ps. 91:4)*

Have you heard of people who proclaim they talk with angels? Scripture does not support such conversation or fascination with God's guardians. Be discerning, Satan wears angelic disguises. Our attention is to be reserved for Christ Jesus.

> *And no marvel; for Satan himself is transformed into an angel of light. (2 Cor. 11:14)*

> *Let no man beguile you of your reward in voluntary humility and worshipping of angels, intruding into those things which he hath not seen, vainly puffed up by his fleshy mind. (Col. 2:18)*

We are wise to discard interest in things competing with our trust in Christ. Keep the order of creation straight. Ministering spirits serve God by assisting us. Awareness of angel armies need only pad our hearts with comfort. May we strive to be more like Elisha when anxious moments arise. He was familiar with the miraculous. Elisha knew God wouldn't leave him alone in the battle. Let us also share his deep comprehension of Christ's care.

> *Are they not all ministering spirits, sent forth to minister for them who shall be heirs of salvation? (Heb. 1:14)*

And he answered, Fear not: for they that be with us are more than they that be with them. And Elisha prayed, and said, LORD, I pray thee, open his eyes, that he may see. And the Lord opened the eyes of the young man; and he saw: and, behold, the mountain was full of horses and chariots of fire round Elisha. (2 Kings 6:16-17)

Bury any notion stating the Heavenly Father neglects to protect us. We are far from alone in our fears. When the Word of Christ speaks, fear will fall at our side. We will be in safe keeping as God arises in the winds and chariots of angels are called to serve our wars.

There shall no evil befall thee, neither shall any plague come nigh thy dwelling. (Ps. 91:10)

A thousand shall fall at thy side, and ten thousand at thy right hand; but it shall not come nigh thee. (Ps. 91:7)

Let God arise, let his enemies be scattered: let them also that hate him flee before him. (Ps. 68:1)

God is ever present when cherubs fly upon the wings of the wind. Capture the vision of our Lord riding upon a cherub. Carrying our great God to heights of victory, far above every fear perturbing our minds.

> *And he rode upon a cherub, and did fly: yea, he did fly upon the wings of the wind. (Ps. 18:10)*

Cherubs hearken to the command of Christ who positions them with prominence. Where are they placed? Guarding the garden's gates and the mercy seat. Hallowed and precious are the assignments of angels. Are you fathoming what grandeur we are also given by our Father?

> *So he drove out the man; and he placed at the east of the garden of Eden Cherubims, and a flaming sword which turned every way, to keep the way of the tree of life. (Gen. 3:24)*

> *So the people sent to Shiloh, that they might bring from thence the ark of the covenant of the LORD of hosts, which dwelleth between the cherubims: and the two sons of Eli, Hophni and Phinehas, were there with the ark of the covenant of God. (1 Sam. 4:4)*

Selah...Heavenly Hosts only guard what holds significance. As precious jewels in His crown, we are forever on God's mind. May we have our eyes opened like the young man whom Elisha encouraged. It is only when the Word enlightens our darkened minds do we let worries rest upon the wings of angels and fly away with Christ.

> *And they shall be mine, saith the LORD of hosts, in that day when I make up my jewels; and I will spare them, as a man spareth his own son that serveth him. (Mal. 3:17)*

Day 16
A Heart of Peace

What condition is your heart in? Maybe it is hurting, fearful, sick, grieving, lonely, apprehensive, deadened, discerning, joyful, peaceful, happy, or oblivious. We use descriptions without giving it much thought to what exactly the heart entails. The heart we are referring to is not our organ, pumping blood. In God's Word it is the inner man or spirit. When our hearts are born into the Kingdom of God, we need to guard them from carnal reasoning. Our intellect must surrender to the Spirit. How this is accomplished is through communion with Christ Jesus. It is His Word which cleanses us. Scripture requests our minds to be renewed daily by God's Word. Think of renewing your mind like restoring an old car. Returning the car to its original condition creates it to shine. Once refurbished, we avoid the dirt roads which would hide its classiness. Don't you agree, keeping our minds clean is more valuable than a classic car? Let's not get stuck in tunnel vision.

A sound heart is the life of the flesh.
(Pr. 14:30)

And be renewed in the spirit of your mind.
(Eph. 4:23)

A cleansing filter is necessary as we encounter routes through evil tunnels. Unbelief begins blowing the dust before us, skewing our vision. We need Jesus to cleanse our conscience and bodies on a regular basis or end up on a deserted road. Re-route your mind to Scripture. A day off can mean a day dullened to the Spirit. Clarity of decision becomes corroded with confusion. Without direction our hearts develop fear. Fear left on cruise will create anxiety. Anxiety is navigating through life with an evil expectation. Now we can see how peace gets left on the wayside. Moments separated from our Savior cost us much peace and life. To indulge in the pride of self-sufficiency dries up our hearts. This is not meant to be a guilt trip into the Word. Please don't approach time spent with Christ Jesus as a task but as a beautiful date basking in His love.

> *Trust in the LORD with all thine heart;*
> *and lean not unto thine own understanding.*
> *(Prov. 3:5)*

> *For to be carnally minded is death; but to be spiritually minded is life and peace. (Rom. 8:6)*

> *That he might sanctify and cleanse it with washing of water by the word. (Eph. 5:26)*

Love from our God drives out fear. Paying heed to the perfect one who provides for our needs brings us to a rest stop. Grace always is received in a humble, resting position. So, shift out of high gear and let God take the wheel. He will lead you into safe zones, away from the pressures causing a traffic jam. You are on a new road to recovery.

> *But he giveth more grace. Wherefore he saith, God resisteth the proud, but giveth grace unto the humble. (James 4:6)*

Jesus will fill the heart's tank. There will be no room for symptoms of panic, immobilization, hiding, lack of concentration, poor performance, addictions, self-mutilation, hair pulling, sickness, over exercising, starvation or anything which muddies your mind. Won't you give the license of your free will to Christ? The road to a diseased heart means we took a detour from the Word. Take Christ as your traveling companion and be on the freeway called life and peace.

Now the Lord of peace Himself give you peace always by all means. The Lord be with you all. (2 Thess. 3:16)

Day 17
Weary? Wear the Right Yoke

What are you working on? Maybe it's your marriage, career, grief, depression, anxiety, home, parenting, minimizing, education, or even faith. Your goal looks quite feasible and noble until weariness sets in. Although you plunged in with admirable commitment, your progress might seem to be set to a turtle's clock. Impatience sets in as you encounter a pool of other problems. Fatigue finds a segue into sadness. Sorrow offers its hand to loneliness. Emptiness lends itself to pity. Pity parties with anger. Animosity aligns with resentment. Bitterness binds the body with sickness. Disease sings the blues to your soul. How did tiredness tether you to such millstones? Most likely it began with your understanding of work. Work excludes the burden when you wear the right yoke.

> *Come unto me, all ye that labour and are heavy laden, and I will give you rest. Take my yoke upon you, and learn of me; for I am meek and lowly in heart: and ye shall find rest for your souls. (Matt. 11:28-29)*

The refreshment for your soul described in the above verse, is a way of life, not just a rest stop when you need a cool drink. Jesus is saying to join Him, and not to rely upon your efforts or the world's methods. Don't be depleted, draw upon the everlasting strength of the Spirit. Immersed in the Holy Spirit means you have put on Christ. Now don't slip off His yoke and take back your problems. Jesus is the main ox pulling the yoke. You are to keep in step with the Spirit.

> *For as many of you as have been baptized into Christ have put on Christ. (Gal. 3:27)*

This is the secret to working without weariness. Rest is more than a nap, it is a state of receiving grace for your daily functioning. In Christ, your work is done out of overflowing strength. All glory then goes to God when your weariness is replaced with His wardrobe.

Day 18

The Traveling Companions of Trouble

Scripture alerts us to a pair of invaders which prey upon our peace. They blaze their trail through sin and unbelief. Roaming the earth, they have devouring eyes upon vulnerable minds. They use the slide of lies to enter our souls. Whispering the way will be unsafe and lonely, the wicked spirits want to weaken our faith. They hope to motor our mouths with confessions of unsettling feelings. Thwarting our proclamation of truth, the thieves disarm the power within us.

> *For with the heart man believeth unto righteousness; and with the mouth confession is made unto salvation. (Rom. 10:10)*

When hearts and mouths are left unguarded, a shipload of trouble can anchor into our souls. Watch for the signs of this couple, for they will stamp footprints of foolishness upon our hearts. The spirits troubling our waters are grief and fear.

> *Whoso keepeth his mouth and his tongue keepeth his soul from troubles. (Prov. 21:23)*

> *Keep thy heart with all diligence; for out of it are the issues of life. (Prov. 4:23)*

Grief and fear are traveling companions looking to conquer our lives. Swiftly it can happen; gladness gives its rights over to grief. Anxiety pushes away God's peace. Hiding under the branches of good and evil, they use the fruits of knowledge to keep us captive. Beware of the Tree of the Knowledge of good and evil. Its conniving fruit tells us we can figure the way out of our problems. We will believe in our skills to pass us through the valleys. Intellectualism permeates a thick fog, perverting all paths to freedom. The Tree of Life becomes hidden by unbelief. Taking the trail with sorrow and fretfulness takes us into the wilderness. In the silence a voice speaks as in the days of John the Baptist, finding our inner chambers. Our hearts tremble with welcoming change.

> *For this is he that was spoken of by the prophet Esaias, saying, The voice of one crying in the wilderness, Prepare ye the way of the Lord, make his paths straight. (Matt. 3:3)*

The Traveling Companions Of Trouble

> *Then shall the lame man leap as an hart, and the tongue of the dumb sing: for in the wilderness shall waters break out, and streams in the desert. (Is. 35:6)*

The Word we hear sends a cleansing shower upon our minds. Christ drains grief and fear into the dead sea. No longer lost, we flow with rivers of life.

> *Then will I sprinkle clean water upon you, and ye shall be clean: from all your filthiness, and from all your idols, will I cleanse you. (Ezek. 36:25)*

> *He that believeth on me, as the scripture hath said, out of his belly shall flow rivers of living water. (Jn. 7:38)*

Panic flushes out as our hearts pump in new peace. Joy joins in and sorrow jumps out. Miracles of love hold no timetable. We behold the vision of Christ's blood running from Calvary into our veins. His resurrected power has raised us above grief and fear. Our priorities are put back into God's purpose. Freely we walk in God's will as He equips us for our eternal mission. Where are the companions of grief and fear? Stopped at the gate of Heaven, their travel plans are canceled.

And it shall come to pass in the day that the LORD shall give thee rest from thy sorrow, and from thy fear, and from the hard bondage wherein thou wast made to serve. (Is. 14:3)

Then shall the virgin rejoice in the dance, both young men and old together: for I will turn their mourning into joy, and will comfort them, and make them rejoice from their sorrow. (Jer. 31:13)

Day 19
Withered and Weak

Fear soaks up energy like a dry sponge. Understandably so, for anxious thoughts swarm like busy bees day and night leaving a person with no rest. Counting sheep, thought stopping or distraction exercises are worse than calisthenics. Slowing down or ending the activity within the brain is tougher than people realize. If only they knew fretfulness races down its own track, violating all speed limits. Living with anxiety exhausts the inner world; leaving countless lives withered and weak.

Withered and weak minds struggle with a normal day's work. It is like traveling with luggage only known to you. You lug this invisible baggage into stores, workplaces, home, while driving or on vacation. Careful to guard the annoyance from others, you strive hard to accomplish your work. It is annoying to both you and the impatient bystanders who are unaware you are barely keeping up.

Anxiety can tag along with other troublemakers such as attention deficit disorder. Scrambled thoughts and impaired memory disprove you to be responsible and trustworthy. The string of issues seems to be endless. May we please come to the end of the problem and introduce a cure? Your answer is not HOW to cause your broken brain system to become whole, but WHO can perform the surgery. Hand over your state of worry to the surgeon who heals all who ask and believe.

Hand Over Your Worry

Before we learn about our surgeon, take this moment to identify your fears. Write down your worries without any suggestions on how to fix them. Now hand your list over to Jesus. Go ahead, stretch forth your hand and tell Him you are ready for surgery. Now join a disabled man whose hand was capable of only holding fear and grief.

> *And he entered again into the synagogue; and there was a man there which had a withered hand. And they watched him, whether he would heal him on the sabbath day; that they might accuse him. And he saith unto the man which had the withered hand, Stand forth. And he saith unto them, Is it lawful to do good on the sabbath days, or to do evil? to save life, or to kill? But they held their peace. And when he had looked round about on them with anger, being grieved for the hardness of their*

hearts, he saith unto the man, Stretch forth thine hand. And he stretched it out: and his hand was restored whole as the other. (Mark 3:1-5)

As you stand with this man, notice he is not enjoying a good days work or any activities we all take for granted. Holding up a brave front, he cries in private, fearing ridicule, failure, and the future. He goes to the synagogue without knowing he would have an audience. Embarrassed by his withered hand, he probably didn't want the attention. However, he was called out by an attending surgeon. Surgery on the Sabbath Day? Why the laws forbid work to be done. Plus, it wasn't an emergency since the man didn't become withered in a day. Withering takes some time. The weak man was probably hoping there would be an exception to the demands of the law while the Pharisees wanted to accuse the surgeon of wrongdoing. They had no compassion for the man. Impatient and emotionally charged, the crowd was in the waiting room ready for the answer.

The surgeon makes His schedule known. The man's weakness takes precedence over the day of the week. The surgeon stands by His credentials: Savior. Love powers up and performs without an instrument. The withered hand becomes whole. Jesus, the saving surgeon teaches his audience. The new law is to love your neighbor not to leave him weak and withered.

> *A new commandment I give unto you, That ye love one another; as I have loved you, that ye also love one another. (Jn. 13:34)*

You stand in awe as you see the power of love. Could this same power silence your fear and give you a sound mind? As you understand true love the answer will unfold.

> *There is no fear in love; but perfect love casteth out fear: because fear hath torment. He that feareth is not made perfect in love. (1 Jn. 4:18)*

> *For God has not given us the spirit of fear; but of power, and of love, and of a sound mind. (2 Tim. 1:7)*

Jesus sees the doubts swirling through your heart. This is why He gave you, His Word. Salvation comes by hearing His promises. The more you read His love letter the stronger your conviction becomes. His Word is like receiving medicine. Each dose softens hardened hearts. Belief brings His promise to life. Each hesitation has an answer. If in the back of your mind you think a withered hand is more important to Jesus than your worry, you are wrong.

He sent his word, and healed them, and delivered them from their destructions. (Ps. 107:20)

You are Equally Important

Perhaps you believe that someone else's problem overrides your own. Minimizing your problem is a barrier to your healing. I have heard too many people say the Lord doesn't have time for my little worry when there are people with bigger problems. Thinking your concern isn't worth God's attention separates you from grace. His love isn't measured by the size of your burden. You will not receive God's gifts by stepping out of the line of love. Trust Him, for He will never overlook an opportunity to help you.

For there is no respect of persons with God. (Rom. 2:11)

What the verse above means is the Lord provides an equal platform to receive His blessings. Christ Jesus doesn't show favoritism or partiality. Rest assured, any need you deem as large or small is important to Him. It is pertinent to ask and remain in the position of dependence; for only in Him lies restoration for the withered and weary. Therefore, no matter how broken you may feel, Jesus will march in wholeness. Believe for your miracle, Jesus took your bruised mind to the cross. Ready?

Stretch forth your handful of worries and allow Jesus your surgeon to save you.

> *A bruised reed shall he not break, and smoking flax shall he not quench, till he send forth judgment unto victory. (Mt. 12:20)*
>
> *But he was wounded for our transgressions, He was bruised for our iniquities: the chastisement of our peace was upon him; and with his stripes we are healed. (Is. 53:5)*

Day 20
Walls of Protection

In Biblical times walls and gates were significant for protection. Keeping the enemies out required fortitude as well as watchmen to alert impending threats. If the walls became corroded, repairs were immediately made to avoid a breach weakening it for an attack. Followers of Christ Jesus also have walls that need to be watched over. Instead of city walls and gates to protect, we have temples. In Scripture, our bodies are considered temples housing the Holy Spirit. Possessing holy ground within requires ongoing inspection for what condition our walls and gates are in.

> *What? know ye not that your body is the temple of the Holy Ghost which is in you, which ye have of God, and ye are not your own? (1 Cor. 6:19)*

Ponder the purpose for such protectiveness! We house a precious commodity. The Holy Spirit places the Kingdom of God right within our very being!

Moses might have had the privilege of standing on holy ground near the burning bush, but we have holy ground standing within us! This gift is not something we have conjured on our own. It came by a very high price.

> *For ye are bought with a price: therefore glorify God in your body, and in your spirit, which are God's. (1 Cor. 6:20)*

We were bought at a high cost but at times we feel too spent to go on. Why? We either slip into sin or brush up against the unclean society. Both deteriorate and dirty our temples. Our temples require ongoing repair and renewal. After inspecting our need for change, we must never allow condemnation to enter the door. Criticism is a curse and keeps our minds away from Christ Jesus. Simply come to the Savior when the filthy rags hanging in our temples need cleaning. He will get rid of sin's stains while reminding us that His righteousness hasn't been removed. Cleansing doesn't change His love for us. Christ continues to bring us back into the pasture when we stray away into enemy territory.

> *Sanctify them through thy truth: thy word is truth. (Jn. 17:17)*

> *That he might sanctify and cleanse it with the washing of the water by the word. (Eph 5:26)*

Border Control

Christ Jesus is our border control. He is the wall protecting us from enemy attacks or preventing us from wandering into danger. Think of Him as the gatekeeper, permitting only goodness to enter and shutting evil out. When we are in the safety of the Kingdom, we will be fed the finest of wheat. Therefore, when the wolves of this world threaten us, we can shut their mouths by singing *He is the wall of Salvation and Praise in our gates*. Fear cannot enter temples whose borders are secured with God's peace.

> *He maketh peace in thy borders, and filleth thee with the finest of wheat. (Ps. 147:14)*
>
> *Violence shall no more be heard in thy land, wasting nor destruction within thy borders; but thou shalt call they walls Salvation, and thy gates Praise. (Is. 60:18)*
>
> *For he hath strengthened the bars of thy gates; he hath blessed thy children within thee. (Ps. 147:13)*

Day 21
Safe With Your Savior

The horse is prepared against the day of battle: but safety is of the LORD. (Prov. 21:31)

Safety is not a subject highly sought after nor does it lay heavy on many minds. We hear of it most often when obligation ushers us into safety training at our workplace. Organizations set up safety plans and instruct us how to prevent accidents and prepare for disasters. Most often the demonstrations and drills are approached with yawns and drooping eyelids. However, the atmosphere ignites interest when an accident report includes their name. An alarm clock suddenly awakens these sleepwalkers into real time. Unfortunately, personal experience with pain is the catalyst which opens their eyes. Now rather than balking the system, they see their employer is trying to build a safer environment. Have you noticed these end times are also sending our hearts constant alerts? Just turn the television on;

unleashed crime, wars, tornados, hurricanes, and earthquakes force us to pay attention as our basic need for safety is shaken.

> *This know also, that in the last days perilous times shall come. (2 Tim. 3:1)*

What type of response will we have when bullets and bomb threats brush against our gates? Will we rely on the still small voice of God or be like the scarecrow on the Wizard of Oz, standing before the closed curtain in utter fear? Living oblivious to the opposition surrounding us is unwise. Don't be lulled into lavish living which dullens the senses. Discern the day's signs. Perilous times require soul preparation. Open the manual to gain wisdom for when legs give out and minds freeze with fear. The Word of Christ will enlighten our spiritual eyes to the constant care surrounding us.

> *Ye hypocrites, ye can discern the face of the sky and of the earth; but how is it that ye do not discern this time? (Lk. 12:56)*

> *And as it was in the days of Noe, so shall it be also in the days of the Son of Man. They did eat, they drank, they married wives, they were given in marriage, until the day that*

Noe entered into the ark, and the flood came, and destroyed them all. (Lk. 17:26-27)

It is when our vision is limited, fear sets in. Only by the Holy Spirit can our humanity extend to the horizons of fearless faith. Investigating our Savior's provision will equip our hearts with confidence. Knowing God's promises sheds light upon His ways. He will lead with peace so when dark times appear, we can walk by faith, not sight. Trust is deepened when the security lights go out.

> *For ye shall go out with joy, and be led forth with peace: the mountains and the hills shall break forth before you into singing, and all the trees of the field shall clap their hands. (Is. 55:12)*
>
> *For we walk by faith not by sight. (2 Cor. 5:7)*

Can we envision the Heavenly Father initiating His plans for our safety? Sometimes they are recognized, but more often are hidden to the human eye. Our Lord doesn't need an alarm clock or an alert to recognize our needs. Unlike our frail flesh, God doesn't slumber but faithfully guards our lives day and night. Knowing Jesus is near tucks our minds in beds with sweet sleep.

> *Behold, he that keepeth Israel shall neither slumber nor sleep. (Ps. 121:4)*
>
> *I will both lay me down in peace, and sleep: for thou, LORD, only makest me dwell in safety. (Ps. 4:8)*
>
> *When thou liest down, thou shalt not be afraid: yea, thou shalt lie down, and your sleep will be sweet. (Prov. 3:24)*

Anyone battling with anxiety knows it is not only at night the switch in the brain seems broken. Streaming thoughts seamlessly wander into revolving doors of worry. Once swept in, it seems impossible to get out. The worry can deafen the voice of our Savior. Our weak minds can't pay attention to what matters whether it is through distraction or exhaustion. Jesus perceives the problem and heeds us to watch and pray.

> *And he cometh unto the disciples, and findeth them asleep, and saith unto Peter, What, could ye not watch with me one hour? Watch and pray, that ye enter not into temptation: the spirit indeed is willing, but the flesh is weak. (Matt. 26: 40-41)*

As the end draws near, we don't need to develop a lazy eye. Scripture needs to be our focus. How else will we hear God's plans for us? Without hearing His response, we would only be lost, listening to our own cries. There is absolutely no reason for believers to walk this earth in fear when God's protection plan lies before us in print. When we recognize Jesus is the Word, our stance will stay strong as evil days surround us. Why not join me tomorrow when we read through the notorious Psalm of protection. If it isn't already a daily Scripture to recite, please put it into your planner and find the peace it provides.

Day 22
The Psalm of Protection

Speaking Scripture aligns our thoughts and words with heaven. We literally join in the language of the Lord Jesus Christ. Have you ever wondered what is on His mind? Look and see. Inscribed in the pages of the Holy Bible is a portal into the inner chambers of the Fathers' heart. It is in the Word our carnal thoughts become beautifully transformed into the mind of Christ. His faithful promises break the ceiling of our finite vision while faith is birthed. Let us not rush as a mouse scampering for morsels of food as we listen to His voice. Savor the bread that bonds us to the impossible. Each word echoes trust into the canyons of our unbelief, causing us to climb to higher heights. What a privilege to pray His Words and be a part of His grand performance. Psalm 91 holds a myriad of gems and will change cowardice into sparkling confidence in Christ. I challenge you to confess it daily and discover His divine power in your daily walk. Bar none, this practice has proven insurmountable peace in my own life.

Take God at His Word. Picture pesky viruses lying in valleys and violence saluting the Savior. The power of Christ leaves you unscathed. No sneaky snakes or snares will snatch you from safety. The voice of the devil deafens as feathers dust lies off your mind. Fascination with the fearful is left on twitter and talk shows. There is no time to tend to anxiety knowing angels hold you up in their hands and demons are beneath your feet. This secret place is yours because of a Savior who paid your way into His Heavenly provision. Speak the Psalm of protection and share in the mind of Christ.

> *He that dwelleth in the secret place of the most High shall abide under the shadow of the Almighty.*
>
> *I will say of the LORD, He is my refuge and my fortress: my God; in him will I trust.*
>
> *Surely he shall deliver thee from the snare of the fowler, and from the noisome pestilence.*
>
> *He shall cover thee with his feathers, and under his wings shalt thou trust: his truth shall be thy shield and buckler.*
>
> *Thou shalt not be afraid for the terror by night; nor for the arrow that flieth by day;*

Nor for the pestilence that walketh in darkness; nor for the destruction that wasteth at noonday.

A thousand shall fall at thy side, and ten thousand at thy right hand; but it shall not come nigh thee.

Only with thine eyes shalt thou behold and see the reward of the wicked.

Because thou hast made the LORD, which is my refuge, even the most High, thy habitation;

There shall no evil befall thee, neither shall any plague come nigh thy dwelling.

For he shall give his angels charge over thee, to keep thee in all thy ways.

They shall bear thee up in their hands, lest thou dash thy foot against a stone.

Thou shalt tread upon the lion and adder: the young lion and the dragon shalt thou trample under feet.

Because he hath set his love upon me, therefore will I deliver him: I will set him on high, because he hath known my name.

He shall call upon me, and I will answer him: I will be with him in trouble; I will deliver him, and honour him.

With long life will I satisfy him, and shew him my salvation. (Ps. 91)

Day 23
Complete In Christ

Companionship is at times in competition with our relationship with Christ Jesus. Leaning on the love of another human above God sways our lives. Take this prop away and frantic feelings of being alone find their way into bleeding hearts. Some people describe it as half their heart is ripped out or their right arm is cut off when their spouse dies. Grief can give false impressions and without checking what the written Word says people ignorantly accept them.

My own spouse was recently diagnosed with cancer. The spirit of fear awakened me in the night telling me I would be alone, broke and without housing due to my possession of a big, unsocial German Shepherd. I've learned from Jesus to defend my thoughts with the Word and the devil would have to flee. Putting my book light on, I opened to Isaiah 54: 4-6. It is never a coincidence when I encounter the Holy Word. His truth set me free and sent the spirit of fear away. Warm comfort permeated my mind until fear decided to visit me the next day.

Fear not; for thou shalt not be ashamed: neither be thou confounded; for thou shalt not be put to shame: for thou shalt forget the shame of thy youth, and shalt not remember the reproach of thy widowhood anymore. For thy Maker is thine husband; the LORD of hosts is his name; and thy Redeemer the Holy One of Israel; The God of the whole earth shall he be called. For the LORD hath called thee as a woman forsaken and grieved in spirit, and a wife of youth, when thou wast refused, saith thy God. (Is. 54: 4-6)

The spirit of fear tried to trick me into thinking I would be limping through life without my soulmate. Like I mentioned in the opening paragraph, I have heard people's statements undergoing amputation of arms and hearts. Working in hospice as a bereavement coordinator and chaplain has given me great insight into the souls of grieving people. Common feelings of grief are treated as truth on a silver platter. Because their emotions are serving sadness, anger, confusion, denial or depression, people accept them like daily bread. The great universities that gobbled up my money told me this was the way out of grief. Accept the feelings or the grief journey would be complicated. I am embarrassed to say I took my degree with dignity until I encountered the living Word. With much apology to souls

I misguided, may Jesus show them the error of this teaching. Shake off the dust from our feet and tread upon the serpent that deceives us into sorrow. Let us grow up in faith and feed on Christ, our Heavenly bread. Only Jesus will show us who we are; whole in Him. We were complete in Christ when we were saved whether married or not. A relationship should never be elevated above our Lord and Savior Jesus Christ.

> *And ye are complete in him, which is the head of all principality and power. (Col. 2:10)*
>
> *Thou shalt tread upon the lion and adder: the young lion and the dragon shalt thou trample under feet. (Ps. 91:13)*

A third visit from the devil again tried to tempt me into thinking I would be poor and deprived of proper provision. Swiftly the Holy Spirit reminded me that my income is not derived from a job or spouse. He told me Jesus became poverty to make me rich and my God would supply all my needs according to the glorious riches in Christ Jesus. I was not to worry about tomorrow for I am way more valuable than birds and flowers. Jesus has me covered and complete; and so, He will also be for you.

For ye know the grace of our Lord Jesus Christ, that, though he was rich, yet for your sakes He became poor, that ye through His poverty might be rich. (2 Cor. 8:9)

But my God shall supply all your need according to his riches in glory by Christ Jesus. (Phil. 4:19)

Therefore take no thought, saying, What shall we eat? Or, What shall we drink? Or, Wherewithal shall we be clothed? (For after all these things do the Gentiles seek:) for your heavenly Father knoweth that ye have need of all these things. But seek ye first the kingdom of God, and his righteousness; and all these things shall be added unto you. Take therefore no thought for the morrow: for the morrow shall take thought for the things of itself. Sufficient unto the day is the evil thereof. (Matt. 6:31-34)

When the spirit of fear frolics with our minds, we are to quickly ignore it and speak the Scriptures. Don't let the devil have a say; for he can only squirm his way into our lives through falsehood. The future holds greatness no matter what our status in life is. We need not be overcome with our faltering feelings when God has overcome the world. Our purpose is to present the world with the Gospel and not to give glory to grief and fear. Never forget, God wants us whole; for He has not created us to be half a human. Our completion is not found in other people, but in Christ alone. Now may we proceed to finish our calling; for the glory of the Lord lives in us.

> *For whatsoever is born of God overcometh the world: and this is the victory that overcometh the world, even our faith. (1 Jn. 5:4)*

Day 24
Christ Esteem

Wondering what people think of you? Feeling inept in the workplace? Maybe family members have standards that don't align with yours. Sometimes it does appear that nobody is on your side. Lonely and low is a horrible place to be. Measuring self-worth with human standards only shatters the confidence.

Struggling with self-esteem is an overpowering problem. It hinders personal and professional development and hides people in the shadows of success. Counselors recommend speaking affirmations in the mirror to convince clients they are accepted. The exercise may reflect a moment of assent until opposition cracks their glass.

Digging into the core of self-love doesn't offer sufficient deliverance. Right standing with others or self won't be discovered by looking horizontally or within, but up. Freedom from condemnation comes only from Christ Jesus. You see, the contention lies in reconciling imperfect with perfect. No human on earth is flawless.

Think about it, the people who are snubbing you must wipe the fog off their own marred perceptions.

> *But why dost thou judge thy brother? or why dost thou set at nought thy brother? for we shall all shall stand before the judgment seat of Christ. (Rom. 14:10)*

> *There is therefore now no condemnation to them which are in Christ Jesus, who walk not after the flesh, but after the Spirit. (Rom. 8:1)*

The answer to acceptance is not in mirrors held by you or others. It is in the heart of the Father. The judgment staring back at you has been removed. When the Father sent His Son to rescue you from your sins, He set you free from the self-worth war. Your worth is not based upon your performance but in the sacrifice of Jesus Christ. Stop staring at yourself and others. Direct your gaze upon grace which grants you acceptance with God. Right standing before the Father has been established already. His approval rating is far more pertinent than any other.

> *For all have sinned, and come short of the glory of God; Being justified freely by his grace through the redemption that is in Christ Jesus: Whom God hast set forth to be*

a propitiation through faith in his blood, to declare his righteousness for the remission of sins that are past, through the forbearance of God. (Rom. 3:23-25)

What does grace make you? Loved, cherished, respected, admired, valued and worthy in the Heavenly Father's eyes. Please, put that mirror down and look up. Your self-esteem has become Christ esteem. Without knowing, you are reflecting the glory of God. Now move ahead and pursue your personal or professional plans. What can people do to you when you have the Lord on your side?

And as we have borne the image of the earthly, we shall also bear the image of he heavenly. (1 Cor. 15:49)

The LORD is on my side; I will not fear: what can man do unto me? (Ps. 118:6)

What shall we then say to these things? If God be for us, who can be against us? (Rom. 8:31)

Day 25
Difficult Decisions

Do you have a difficult time making decisions? If so, look out for the opponent who is proposing you with fear. The enemy coming against your choice doesn't want you to proceed forward. Fear poses all the possibilities for your failure, immobilizing your next move. It blends gloom and doom into your thinking while shutting the door to your confidence. Even scribbling choices onto a notepad becomes useless. Anxiety just keeps erasing your vision for victory. Fellow believer, you are not the loser in this game. You need to know the devil will keep batting you balls of fear until you learn not to catch them. Get ready for a new game plan. With God you will be overrunning the base of confusion onto a home run.

> *For God is not the author of confusion, but of peace, as in all the churches of the saints. (1 Cor. 14:33)*

Resetting Priorities

Putting a plan into place requires resetting your priorities. Many go wrong by soaking their decisions in raw emotion or forthright intelligence. Either approach is a risky strategy. Sole reliance upon the carnal mind places you into the playing field of Satan. His kingdom lures the lustful flesh to wear mitts holding pride. It is an easy slide into selfish gain when the score board flashes success. Running home with worldliness won't give you peace. Why such unrest? Refusing God's wisdom results in a ruffled heart. The omission of God will keep you chasing balls in the outfield. Take a knee and listen to the wisdom which will change your game.

> *For the LORD giveth wisdom: out of his mouth cometh knowledge and understanding. (Prov. 2:6)*

Faith Versus Intellect

Gods' wisdom is different from human knowledge. Too often Christians mistakenly listen to their intellectual reasoning. Where does the intellect draw its information? It works in direct relation to the five senses: eyes, ears, smell, touch, and taste. Intellectual reasoning relates to the physical world in this manner, but we believers have so much more than this. While we are aware of our five senses, we do not rely upon them when making decisions. Our lives are in connection with Christ Jesus, who is Spirit. Our spirits are to be led by faith, not the five senses. This is why the written Word is to be valued. Christians listen to the voice of God because our minds are renewed. Renewed means our minds are born into God's kingdom. They have changed uniforms, due to submission in Christ. Therefore, we move within the context of the spiritual realm.

> *But the natural man receiveth not the things of the Spirit of God: for they are foolishness unto him: neither can he know them, because they are spiritually discerned. But he that is spiritual judgeth all things, yet he himself is judged of no man. For who hath known the mind of the Lord, that he may instruct him? But we have the mind of Christ. (1 Cor. 2:14-16)*

> *Howbeit we speak wisdom among them that are perfect: yet not the wisdom of this world, nor the princes of this world, that come to nought: But we speak the wisdom of God in a mystery, even the hidden wisdom, which God ordained before the world unto our glory: Which none of the princes of this world knew: for had they known it, they would not have crucified the Lord of glory. (1 Cor. 2:6-8)*

And be not conformed to this world: but be ye transformed by the renewing of your mind, that ye may prove what is that good, and acceptable, and perfect, will of God. (Rom. 12:2)

And be renewed in the spirit of your mind. (Eph. 4:23)

Line Up with the Lord

Before you run with a decision, search out Scripture. Proceeding to the next base with mere facts, leads to a loss. Make sure you line up with the Lord Jesus Christ. For example, while seeking employment, would you accept the job if the income slams a home run but insists you wear the uniform of immorality? What goal is worth your cause? If you don't know the answer, there is a flag thrown before your feet. Stop all action and consult with the Lord. There is more NO in "I don't k**no**w" than yes. Your next step requires wisdom not found in your five senses, but in the inspiration of Scripture. Christ will put your feet into play with a plan written in peace.

But as it is written, Eye hath not seen, nor ear heard, neither have entered into the heart of man, the things which God hath prepared for them that love him. But God hath revealed them unto us by his Spirit: for the Spirit searcheth all things, yea, the deep things of God. (1 Cor. 2:9-10)

For to be carnally minded is death; but to be spiritually minded is life and peace. (Rom. 8:6)

He layeth up sound wisdom for the righteous: he is a buckler to them that walk uprightly. He keepeth the paths of judgment, and preserveth the way of his saints. Then shalt thou understand righteousness, and judgment, and equity; yea, every good path. (Prov. 2:7-9)

Peace in the Plan

Your game plan may not make sense to others but trust the Spirit's guidance. God will speak to you through His Spirit in His written Word. There will be a confirming peace as He directs your decisions. You are not alone; the Holy Spirit will assist you along the Father's path.

Now we have received, not the spirit of the world, but the spirit which is of God; that we might know the things that are freely given to us of God. Which things also we speak, not in the words which man's wisdom teacheth, but which the Holy Ghost teacheth; comparing spiritual things with spiritual. (1 Cor. 2:12-13)

Thou wilt shew me the path of life: in thy presence is fulness of joy; at thy right hand there are pleasures for evermore. (Ps. 16:11)

Her ways are ways of pleasantness, and all her paths are peace. (Prov. 3:17)

Walk into His Will

Trust the Lord to walk you into His will. Are you still scared you might make a mistake? Listen to the still small voice of His Spirit. He will nudge you with a grudging if you are taking a wrong turn. You have unseen backup. Jesus is behind the scenes, praying on your behalf! He is watching your every move and will warn you of upcoming danger.

And thine ears shall hear a word behind thee, saying, This is the way, walk ye in it, when ye turn to the right hand, and when ye turn to the left. (Is. 30:21)

Difficult Decisions

Out of the Field of Evil

Executing your plan through wisdom keeps you out of the field of evil. You can't go wrong when Jesus is interceding on your behalf. Your responsibility is to pay attention to God's Son, not the devil shouting "loser" into your ears.

> *I pray not that thou shouldest take them out of the world, but that thou shouldest keep them from the evil. (Jn. 17:15)*

> *Wherefore he is able also to save them to the uttermost that come unto God by him, seeing he ever liveth to make intercession for them. (Heb. 7:25)*

Dare to Decide

Finally, you can come to terms with a plan. With your eye on the Word, floodlights of fear will shatter. You will see Jesus holding your hand. He will be like the dawn, beckoning new light on your choices. It all transpires beyond your understanding. Walking in His peace, a guard is placed over your mind and heart. Ready for the game? Get out of the dugout and dare to make that decision.

Trust in the LORD with all thine heart; and lean not unto thine own understanding. In all thy ways acknowledge him, and he shall direct thy paths. Be not wise in thine own eyes: fear the LORD and depart from evil. It shall be health to thy navel, and marrow to thy bones. (Prov. 3:5-8)

Fear thou not; for I am with thee: be not dismayed; for I am thy God: I will strengthen thee; yea, I will help thee; yea, I will uphold thee with the right hand of my righteousness. (Is. 41:10)

And the peace of God, which passeth all understanding, shall keep your hearts and minds through Christ Jesus. (Phil. 4:7)

Day 26

Torment in the Night

Have you ever jolted out of blissful slumber in sheer panic? Without warning, an unseen enemy pounces upon your pillow declaring war. Arrows of anxiety shoot into your mind. They wound you with loaded questions of *what ifs* and *what now?* Regrets are regurgitated and you want to vomit out your poor choices. In a blink of an eye, condemnation chars your character like wildfire. Barely able to breathe, your paralyzed body melts into the mattress. Stuck between the sheets of worry and self-hatred, you are swept into insomnia. An unsettling presence raises the hairs on the back of your neck. Feeling foolishly helpless, you second guess your sanity. Before you check yourself into a psyche ward, lend your ear to hear what the Word says about your experience.

> *Be sober, be vigilant; because your adversary the devil, as a roaring lion, walketh about, seeking whom he may devour: Whom resist stedfast in the faith, knowing that the same*

*afflictions are accomplished in your brethren
that are in the world. (1 Pet. 5:8-9)*

What really snuck into your slumber is an evil spirit. If the subject causes you to shudder, re-examine your belief. Fearing the devil would deem him more powerful than Christ Jesus. The conquest with evil is over and the cross proves it. You are not to be hiding under quilts sewn in fear during this night war. Has the Father not equipped you with His Word? Now put His weapon to work. Interrupt the interrogation and shield yourself with truth. You can go back to sleep knowing this enemy is slain.

> *Above all, taking the shield of faith, wherewith ye shall be able to quench all the fiery darts of the wicked. (Eph. 6:16)*
>
> *Is not my Word like as a fire? saith the LORD; and like a hammer that breaketh the rock in pieces? (Jer. 23:29)*
>
> *By the word of truth, by the power of God, by the armour of righteousness on the right hand and on the left. (2 Cor. 6:7)*

Your good night's rest will return. Just cover your mind with God's Word and close your eyes. Christ Jesus will silence this intruder and send him away. Those dark thoughts of torment will leave when perfect love puts His light on.

> *There is no fear in love; but perfect love casteth out fear: because fear hath torment. He that feareth is not made perfect in love. (1 Jn. 4:18)*

Day 27
Sleep Encounters

Yesterday we addressed the affliction of thoughts tormenting our night. Today we will investigate both pleasant and unpleasant sleep encounters. Drawing upon personal experience, nighttime does not have to equal dread. There have been times I was awakened with utter terror clawing into my bones. Unable to move or speak, a presence held me captive in my bed. After numerous nights of attacks, I was able to whisper the name of Jesus and to my relief, the smothering presence left. The name of Jesus sends evil into the abyss.

> *Then a spirit passed before my face; the hair of my flesh stood up. (Job 4:15)*

> *My bones are pierced in me in the night season: and my sinews take no rest. (Job 30:17)*

And the seventy returned again with joy, saying, Lord, even the devils are subject unto us through thy name. (Lk. 10:17)

Nightmares

Another type of fearful encounter is a nightmare. When having a bad dream, I often find myself to be immobilized and desperate to scream, but my mouth is on mute. While my screams are silenced in the dream, in real time I awaken my husband with shrilling cries for help. I have since learned to pray God's promises before I go to bed. When I remember to do this, His Word guards me from these spirits while I slumber.

In thoughts from the visions of the night, when deep sleep falleth on men, Fear came upon me, and trembling, which made all my bones to shake. (Job 4:13-14)

Warnings

Some dreams warn of upcoming danger. Often, these dreams are reoccurring and place a burden upon the heart. When this occurs, pray for discernment, and spend time in the Word for clarification. While these dreams present impending concern, they don't attack the soul, but fill us with urgency and direction.

For God speaketh once, yea twice, yet man perceiveth it not. In a dream, in a vision of the night, when deep sleep falleth upon men, in slumberings upon the bed; Then he openeth the ears of men, and sealeth their instruction. (Job 33:14-16)

And being warned of God in a dream that they should not return to Herod, they departed into their own country another way. (Mt.2:12)

Reassuring Dreams

Some dreams bring heavenly love onto earth. Once I dreamed, I was dancing in a flowing white gown with Jesus. I awoke with insurmountable joy! It was so majestic I thought I could climb Jacob's ladder.

And he dreamed, and behold a ladder set up on the earth, and the top of it reached to heaven: and behold the angels of God ascending and descending on it. (Gen. 28:12)

Another dream spoke to my fear of car crashes. At 17 years of age, I was a passenger in a serious accident which totaled the car and should have taken all our lives. I struggled with PTSD and drove any driver crazy with my panic during inclement weather. The Lord gave me a dream that my car was crashing into a tree. Before impact, I was released from my body and exited to heaven. Unharmed and without fear, I knew there would be no pain when leaving this earth!

I will conclude with one more dream which replaced fear with confidence. My family put me on downhill skis around the age four. The bunny hill was not an issue for me until our school offered ski lessons. I qualified for the big hills which took me off the tow rope and sent me onto the chairlift. My group was accustomed to the intermediate level while I was not. I felt pushed beyond my capabilities as I struggled to keep up with more experienced skiers. I was instilled with crazy anxiety which hung in my heart for years. One day I was working at the ski hill, and I decided to take the challenge. Back to skiing the big hills. The night before, the Lord gave me a dream that I was flying down the slopes, free as an angel. The following day the dream was fulfilled. Fear forgot to bring its skis and I confidently went down the slopes!

There are dreams remaining without interpretation. I have learned to write them down and patiently wait until the revelation comes. Not every dream is from the Lord. However, when they arrive, they speak deeply like a roaring waterfall. How comforting to know our Father works day and night, straightening the crooked pathways in our minds. When our thinking becomes infested with fear, He filters it out, even through the means of a dream.

> *Deep calleth unto deep at the noise of thy waterspouts: all thy waves and thy billows are gone over me. (Ps. 42:7)*

> *I will go before thee, and make the crooked places straight: I will break in pieces the gates of brass, and cut in sunder the bars of iron. (Is. 45:2)*

Sweet Sleep

> *When I lie down, I say, When shall I arise, and the night be gone? and I am full of tossings to and fro unto the dawning of the day. (Job 7:4)*

What do we do when we dread putting on pajamas? We know insomnia is at our bedside holding our robe and slippers. What we don't want to do is ingest sleeping pills. Instead, please rely upon Jesus, for sweet sleep is another one of His promises. Upon the untimely arrival of insomnia, immediately read or listen to the Word. Restlessness will release us to a divine date with Jesus. Special time with our Savior, even in the night hours, invigorates us for the next day.

*Consider how I love thy precepts: quicken me,
O LORD, according to thy lovingkindness.
(Ps. 119:159)*

*Mine eyes prevent the night watches, that I
might meditate in thy word. (Ps. 119:148)*

*When thou liest down, thou shalt not be
afraid: yea, thou shalt lie down, and thy
sleep shall be sweet. (Prov. 3:24)*

One parting thought before falling asleep. We must remember the battle is not ours to fight. When wicked spirits want to visit us at night, let the Word go to war.

Fighting From Victory

There is power in God's promises. His Word fiercely defends us. We must not keep our Bibles on nightstands unopened. Promises are to be believed, received, and acted upon. One grave error is when we undermine and underutilize our weapon. Strongholds overpowering our sleep are slain with the sword of the Spirit. Don't be misled, when we speak the Word, we fight from victory. The Word simply reminds the wicked one Christ Jesus demolished him. There is no need to get worked up in believing we fight the devil. Pay him no respect, for attention upon him darkens our minds. We are overcomers only because God is abiding in us. From now on, approach bedtime without dreading the devil. Our Father will favor us with a good night's sleep.

> *For the word of God is quick, and powerful, and sharper than any twoedged sword, piercing even to the dividing asunder of soul and spirit, and of the joints and marrow, and is a discerner of the thoughts and intents of the heart. (Heb. 4:12)*

> *I have written unto you, fathers, because ye have known him that is from the beginning. I have written unto you, young men, because ye are strong, and the word of God abideth in you, and ye have overcome the wicked one. (1 Jn. 2:14)*

> *Ye are of God, little children, and have overcome them: because greater is he that is in you, than he that is in the world. (1 Jn. 4:4)*

A Good Night

Good night my dear friend. Place your head on the pillow of grace. Rest, for Jesus is tucking you into His presence. Enjoy sweet sleep as your Savior shelters you from every terror in the night.

Thou shalt not be afraid for the terror by night; nor the arrow that flieth by day. (Ps. 91:5)

In righteousness shalt thou be established: thou shalt be far from oppression; for thou shalt not fear: and from terror, for it shall not come near thee. (Is. 54:14)

Day 28

A Destination Wedding

It is quite popular to host destination weddings. Investing time, travel and funds into the perfect place is fine, unless it overrides the meaning of the ceremony. Strip away the fun, food and drinks and examine the sacred occasion. Will the marriage endure its vows? Deteriorating values are redefining the commitment between couples. When the relationship dissolves into a lukewarm glass of glitz and glamour, the soul sinks into deep depression. Sensing something is amiss, fear dives in and taints their hearts with desperation. Grasping for more gets them nowhere. Adding more to the occasion doesn't resolve this couple's unrest. Lack of peace agitates doubt into their decision to marry. Such chasm breaks the rings attempting to interlock their lives. Without invitation, an unwelcomed guest slips in. Building a wall of silence, the enemy separates their hearts. Weeping overcomes joy as the wedding plans are spoiled. Deception domineers whenever thy first love is disregarded.

> *Nevertheless I have somewhat against thee, because thou hast left thy first love. (Rev. 2:4)*

When plans eliminate Christ Jesus, a disappointing destination prevails. If you want to know what fear to fear, it is not being on the guest list of the wedding feast to come.

Your Bridegroom is Calling

You probably will agree, our society is lovesick. Caught up in the competition and cares of this world serves dissatisfaction into the soul. Searching to fill this heart's vacuum with anything other than God is adultery. His invitation is written in the Holy Bible; true love is calling. Receiving or rejecting the voice of the bridegroom determines the ultimate destination. When the bridegroom comes, the bride will be unveiled for the world to view. Believers will join the wedding song while dark loneliness will loom in unsaved hearts.

> *The voice of joy, and the voice of gladness, the voice of the bridegroom, and the voice of the bride, the voice of them that shall say, Praise the LORD of hosts: for the LORD is good; for his mercy endureth for ever: and of them that shall bring the sacrifice of praise into the house of the LORD. For I will*

> *cause to return the captivity of the land, as at the first, saith the LORD. (Jer. 33:11)*

> *And the light of a candle shall shine no more at all in thee; and the voice of the bridegroom and of the bride shall be heard no more at all in thee: for thy merchants were the great men of the earth; for by thy sorceries were all nations deceived. (Rev. 18:23)*

If loneliness and fear have tied a lasso around your heart, say yes to His proposal. Walk with Jesus who opens the door into everlasting love. You won't be disappointed in this destination wedding.

> *Behold, I stand at the door, and knock: if any man hear my voice, and open the door, I will come in to him, and will sup with him, and he with me. (Rev. 3:20)*

> *And I will satiate the soul of the priests with fatness, and my people shall be satisfied with my goodness, saith the Lord. (Jer. 31:14)*

Our next wedding devotion summons us to behold Solomon and the wedding banquet in Matthew 22. The occasion renders fear powerless and speechless! Come witness fear shutting its mouth as the sword shines truth into the face of evil.

Day 29
The Wedding Without Fear

Marriage is highly esteemed by our Heavenly Father, the originator of love. He illustrates holy matrimony as Jesus the bridegroom, and the church His bride. This demonstrates the intimacy our Father longs to have with His people. With an unquenchable love, He is never distant, or uncaring but filled with adoration for us all. Our Father is so in love with us that He is preparing a special wedding celebration upon His Son's return.

> *Again, he sent forth other servants, saying, Tell them which are bidden, Behold, I have prepared my dinner: my oxen and my fatlings are killed, and all things are ready: come unto the marriage. (Matt. 22:4)*

> *Many waters cannot quench love, neither can the floods drown it: neither can the floods drown it: if a man would give all*

the substance of his house for love, it would utterly be contemned. (Song of Sol. 8:7)

What could the significance of a wedding have to do with fear? Allow Scripture to answer through the eyes of Solomon and Matthew.

Solomon Means Peace

Journey to the 3rd chapter in the Song of Solomon. Keep one eye on this notable king as a type of Christ. The day of espousals emulates our relationship with our Lord. What typically goes with a wedding? Gladness! Our union brings much happiness into the heart of the Father.

> *Go forth, O ye daughters of Zion, and behold king Solomon with the crown wherewith his mother crowned him in the day of his espousals, and in the day of the gladness of his heart. (Song of Sol. 3:11)*

Any day that incorporates gladness is void of fear. One cannot be happy and fearful at the same time. There is nothing disturbing Solomon's wedding. The ceremony was well secured. We know if we eliminate security, evil enters the scene. Therefore, Solomon, whose name means peace, was more than prepared.

Swords On Their Thighs

Solomon had secured his premises with swords. Imagine attending a wedding with men wearing swords on their thighs! He wasn't overprotective for there was good reason for such attire. Scripture says it was *because of fear in the night*.

> *They all hold swords, being expert in war: every man hath his sword upon his thigh because of fear in the night. (Song of Sol. 3:8)*

Scripture interprets Scripture; therefore, night or darkness represents the wrath or judgment of God. During the crucifixion daylight turns into night (See Matt.27:45), and on judgment day the moon will turn to blood and the sun will be darkened. (See Joel 2:31). Solomon's security kept the fear in the night (judgment) from intruding upon his sacred ceremony. Our relationship with the Father is also kept from His wrath on judgment day. Scripture states God's wrath was appeased by the sacrifice of His Son. The cross prepared the way for the union with His bride. We know King Jesus cleansed the church on mount Calvary. So too the reference of myrrh on the mountain signifies Solomon's bride was prepared to meet her bridegroom.

Until the day break, and the shadows flee away, I will get me to the mountain of myrrh and to the hill of frankincense. Thou art all fair, my love; there is no spot in thee. (Song of Sol. 4:6-7)

Why the Battle with Fear?

If the bride (church) is prepared and protected from judgment, why do our hearts still fear? Simply stated, we have forgotten our swords. The sword, the Word of God, reminds us of grace and defends us against condemnation. Therefore, we must bear the sword of the Spirit when our minds are battered, and our heart's security is breached.

And take the helmet of salvation, and the sword of the Spirit, which is the word of God. (Eph. 6:17)

This point takes us to the book of Matthew where a security breach occurred. We will witness how an unwelcomed wedding guest was handled.

Onto The Wedding Banquet in Matthew

In Matthew's account of the wedding banquet, the king noticed a bystander who was not properly dressed. Addressing the man as friend, (Jesus came to save all)

The Wedding Without Fear

the king asked how he entered without having a wedding garment. His response? Nothing. The unwelcomed guest was speechless. He couldn't banter or bully the king with excuses but was banished from the banquet.

No one can come into the presence of the Father unless they are robed with Christ's righteousness. Sin's nakedness must be clothed with the forgiveness of Jesus Christ. Do you see what happens when our sinless God meets sin? Unless covered in the blood of His Son, it is escorted into damnation and darkness.

Read Matthew's account below. The unwelcomed guest had nothing to say as he is sent to hell. How does this apply to our fear? Far removed is our judgment and any enemy trying to interfere with our wedding to the King. We don't have to debate any devil wandering into our minds with fear but can shut its mouth with the Word of Christ.

> *And when the king came in to see the guests, he saw there a man which had not on a wedding garment: And he saith unto him, Friend, how camest thou in hither not having a wedding garment? And he was speechless. Then said the king to the servants, Bind him hand and foot, and take him away, and cast him into outer darkness; there shall be weeping and gnashing of teeth. For many are called, but few are chosen. (Matt. 22:11-14)*

Drawing Conclusions

Let's draw the curtain on this amazing wedding scene and come to some conclusions. First, don't allow an unwelcomed guest into our hearts. The enemy will try to disrupt our relationship with God. Second, forbid to dine and dance with an enemy. He will feed us with lies and whisper dark messages into our ears. Feast only with King Jesus. Third, don't forget where we sit. We aren't the ones facing judgment's door. We are seated with the King who is preparing us a remarkable banquet.

Day 30

Are Grief and Fear Weaving a Wall Around your Heart?

Grief and fear are like a woven basket. Hooking people with messages from the abyss, they weave walls around their hearts. The pattern they follow develops feeble minds. Grief and fear choose people who encounter loss. As soon as the fuzzy comforters are gone, they move in with negative news. They wait to see if the bad report makes it to the mind. If it does, they can find their way to weaken the heart. Next fear latches on, tying a tight knot on their lives.

We can glean wisdom from Jeremiah, the weeping prophet, whose life was submerged with seasons of loss. He was keenly aware of how hearts can become faint and fearful when exposed to bad news.

And lest your heart faint, and ye fear for the rumour that shall be heard in the land; a

*rumour shall both come one year, and after
that in another year shall come a rumour,
and violence in the land, ruler against ruler.
(Jer. 51:46)*

With all his warnings to God's people, Jeremiah gives heed to the condition of their hearts. We too need to watch over our hearts when something or someone is stripped away. Grief can take our hearts into hard bondage. It begins with questioning God. During loss, the mind wants to rationalize the "whys". When answers aren't found, loss of control waltzes in. People are disturbed when they don't have a direct hand in their destiny. The bowl of unknowns is good at whipping up a batch of worry. The product is a damaged heart. Therefore, trying to make sense of loss can divert our devotion from Christ. This may be why Jeremiah didn't want any negative news competing with their faith.

*Trust in the LORD with all thine heart;
and lean not unto thine own understanding.
In all thy ways acknowledge him, and he
shall direct thy paths. (Prov. 3:5-6)*

A bad report, whether true or not, can wear us down. Fretting over our circumstances lends to forgetting God's graciousness. Therefore, when surrounded with grief, God's Word can serve to buffer us. Sorrow and worry can't drive in stakes within God's perimeters.

Recognizing we dwell within borders of copious provision, our walls of fear come down. We can tell our troubled hearts; *devastation doesn't equal God's departure.* Yes, loss does change circumstances, but our peace remains. Shall we look at the bigger picture? The barrier of fear was demolished when Jesus died on the cross. He demolished the wall separating us from all the Father's promises.

> *For he is our peace, who hath made both one, and hath broken down the middle wall of partition between us. (Eph. 2:14)*
>
> *And, behold, the veil of the temple was rent in twain from the top to the bottom; and the earth did quake, and the rocks rent. (Matt. 27:51)*

Drawing our Conclusion

The wall weaved by grief and fear has fallen. Therefore, loss can't separate us from our Father. He did not design our heart for fear or grief, but for His peace. Bad news does not have to entwine our hearts with sorrow or fretfulness ever again.

Day 31
Work Doesn't Define Your Worth

Have you ever felt you were in an interview upon meeting someone new? Somewhere in the agenda springs a question regarding work or education. The tone shifts from sharing information to a competition. The conversation seems to have driven you to a swim meet. Performance now competes with your identity. Your stomach begins to churn, and you feel uncomfortably inadequate. Stop this meeting of minds before you jump off the diving board of judgment. In the waters below, productivity is racing to redefine the meaning of your worth. It has its own set of standards which are work based. What happens when people are no longer swimming and are on the sidelines? Failure to succeed generates fear when the world's math states underachievement equals worthlessness. It is this mentality that multiplies regrets. Such beliefs should be fed to the sharks. Wading in these shallow minds is a society defining our success with status. Paddle past the devilish concepts which want to define your standards and direct your decisions. Instead, set yourself apart for a more meaningful meeting. Do this by diving deep into the words of an Old Testament prophet.

The Old Testament prophets speak to an audience in their era, but the inspiration of the Holy Spirit will reach the ears of your heart as well. Hearken to a personal message from the Father through the mouth of Haggai. You will regain vision of what true prosperity is according to God's terms, not the world's. To labor for a notable reputation, riches or possessions is not on Haggai's docket. While work is included, it is not the object lesson. Productive work will follow when the Holy Spirit aligns your heart with the Father's priorities. His love always underlines His prosperous ways. Hang on, Haggai has these beautiful truths to bathe your heart in.

The Heart of Haggai

Haggai's passionate heart heralds God's Word to Zerubbabel, the governor of Judah and Joshua, the high priest.

> *In the second year of Darius the king, in the sixth month, in the first day of the month, came the word of the LORD by Haggai the prophet unto Zerubbabel the son of Shealtiel, governor of Judah, and to Joshua*

the son of Josedech, the high priest, saying. (Haggai 1:1)

Haggai will plead the importance of spirit directed activity. After Solomon's temple was destroyed by Nebuchadnezzar, two prophets were sent to encourage the people with the news that it was time to rebuild. Haggai and Zechariah were raised up by God to ignite revival in stagnant hearts. The time was ripe. The political situation changed. God's people were released from Babylonian captivity. While some chose to remain in the Babylonian region, others returned to their homeland. Those who sought pilgrimage found the Holy temple was left in shambles. God's people had begun its reconstruction project under Cyrus, king of Persia but only the foundation of the temple was laid. (See Ezra 3:8-13) Opposition from outside rulers stopped their work. (Ezra 4:24) However, during the era of Haggai, there was no excuse. Even though there were still naysayers on site, the building permit was upheld in new hands. (Ezra 6)

Permission Granted

Under new leadership, King Darius granted permission for the temple project to rebegin. Unfortunately, this good news did not generate much interest. Sidetracked by self-interest, God's people who came out from captivity into freedom were busy establishing their own homes. This practical distraction kept them from a heavenly meeting. There was one obstacle; the meeting place wasn't complete. How grieved our Lord must have been to see the ruins within His people's hearts were also needing repair. The Father sincerely missed His children and would do everything He could to bring them back to His side.

> *Thus speaketh the LORD of hosts, saying, This people say, The time is not come, the time that the Lord's house should be built. Then came the word of the Lord by Haggai the prophet saying, Is it time for you, O ye, to dwell in your cieled houses, and this house lie waste? Now therefore thus saith the LORD of hosts; Consider your ways. (Haggai 1:2-5)*

We can identify with the climate of this culture. There is nothing new under the sun when it comes to sin. How many of us are doing the backstroke when Jesus is offering His grace. Let us be the ones to call believers out of lukewarm waters. This generation needs to find God's blueprint and forsake worldly endeavors. It is time to rebuild upon the Father's foundation.

> *Nevertheless the foundation of God standeth sure, having this seal, The Lord knoweth them that are his. And, Let every*

one that nameth the name of Christ depart from iniquity. (2 Tim. 2:19)

I know thy works, that thou art neither cold nor hot: I would thou wert cold or hot. So then because thou art lukewarm, and neither cold nor hot, I will spue thee out of my mouth. Because thou sayest, I am rich and increased with goods, and have need of nothing; and knowest not that thou art wretched, and miserable, and poor, and blind, and naked: I counsel thee to buy of me gold tried in the fire, that thou mayest be rich; and white raiment, that thou mayest be clothed, and that the shame of thy nakedness do not appear, and anoint thine eyes with eye-salve, that thou mayest see. As many as I love, I rebuke and chasten: be zealous therefore, and repent. (Rev. 3:15-19)

God's Priorities Bring Prosperity

Haggai's exhortation to consider their ways was for their own good. He pointed out there was no ultimate satisfaction by the way they were conducting business. They were living impoverished lives. He wanted to elevate them from living beneath God's best.

Work Doesn't Define Your Worth

> *Ye have sown much, and bring in little; ye eat, but ye have not enough; ye drink, but ye are not filled with drink; ye clothe you, but there is none warm; and he that earneth wages earneth wages to put it into a bag with holes. (Haggai 1:6)*

To rebuild the rubble in their hearts, they needed to return to the temple. The temple was not just a building project, it was a place of contact. The temple was where the Father and His people would commune together. Hearts are renewed and priorities are put back into place in the Holy of Holies. Whenever God's people are in His presence, pleasure and joy reside. Seeking His Kingdom first is the secret to successful lives. (See Matt. 6:33)

> *Thus saith the LORD of hosts; Consider your ways. Go up to the mountain, and bring wood, and build the house; and, I will take pleasure in it, and I will be glorified, saith the LORD. Ye looked for much, and lo, it came to little; and when ye brought it home, I did blow upon it. Why? saith the LORD of hosts. Because of mine house that is waste, and ye run every man unto his own house. (Haggai 1:7-9)*

Blessed are they that dwell in thy house: they will be still praising thee. Selah. (Ps.84:4)

Lay not up for yourselves treasures upon earth, where moth and rust doth corrupt, and where thieves break through and steal: But lay up for yourselves treasures in heaven, where neither moth nor rust doth corrupt, and where thieves do not break through nor steal: For where your treasure is, there will your heart be also. (Matt. 6:19-21)

Summary

Today our meeting with God is not limited to a church building. With the privilege of hosting Him inside our hearts, extends our identity beyond the walls of the workplace and universities!

But this shall be the covenant that I will make with the house of Israel; After those days, saith the LORD, I will put my law in their inward parts, and write it in their hearts; and will be their God, and they shall be my people. (Jer. 31:33)

If we slide into society's expectations for our success, our zest for life will wane. Racing with the world will fade true meaning into the sunset. At the end of the day, we will have missed our meeting. Our Father has created us to be in relationship with Himself. By tending to the temple of our hearts, our culture will see true prosperity is founded in Christ Jesus. Success is not in what we do or what we own, but in what the Father does for and through us. As the Spirit directs our activity, our time and money will be used to glorify God, the source of these treasures. Pray for a heart like Haggai's and invite people to this meeting with our God of grace.

> *How amiable are thy tabernacles, O LORD of hosts! My soul longeth, yea, even fainteth for the courts of the LORD: my heart and my flesh crieth out for the living God. For a day in thy courts is better than a thousand. I had rather be a doorkeeper in the house of my God, than to dwell in the tents of wickedness. (Ps. 84:1-2,10)*

> *And they sang together by course in praising and giving thanks unto the Lord; because he is good, for his mercy endureth for ever toward Israel. And all the people shouted with great shout, when they praised the Lord, because the foundation of the house of the Lord was laid. (Ezra 3:11)*

Day 32

Believe and Receive Healing Like Hezekiah

Hezekiah heard the word that his life was going to abruptly end. We know many people who can relate to his tears or maybe it is you. Labs reporting end stage cancer or other terrible diseases will sadden anyone. It is normal to react with fear, anger, or depression.

> *In those days was Hezekiah sick unto death. And Isaiah the prophet the son of Amoz came unto him, and said unto him, Thus saith the LORD, Set thine house in order: for thou shalt die, and not live. (Is. 38:1)*

What would you do in Hezekiah's situation? After the Novocain of disbelief wears off, your choice of action will prove what is in your heart. May we all respond like Hezekiah. He did only one thing: prayed.

> *Then Hezekiah turned his face toward the wall, and prayed unto the LORD, And said, Remember now, O LORD, I beseech thee, how I have walked before thee in truth and with a perfect heart, and have done that which is good in thy sight. And Hezekiah wept sore. Then came the word of the LORD to Isaiah, saying, Go, and say to Hezekiah, Thus saith the Lord, the God of David thy father, I have heard thy prayer, I have seen thy tears: behold, I will add unto thy days fifteen years. (Is. 38: 2-5)*

The Lord honored Hezekiah's faith and transformed his bitter tears into peace. Promises of love poured forth forgiveness and healing, drowning the corruption of sin and disease.

> *Behold, for peace I had great bitterness: but thou hast in love to my soul delivered it from the pit of corruption: for thou hast cast all my sins behind thy back. (Is. 38:17)*

Salvation includes Healing

Notice Hezekiah's response in the verse below. Does not this confirm our Lord's readiness to save?

> *The LORD **was ready to save me**: therefore we will sing my songs to the stringed instruments all the days of our life in the house of the LORD. (Is. 38:20) (Emphasis mine)*

How beautiful it is to know **the Lord is ready to save**! This is the heartbeat of our Father. Hezekiah was not the first nor the last to know of the complete definition of salvation; Moses also understood.

> *And said, If thou wilt diligently hearken to the voice of the LORD thy God, and wilt do that which is right in his sight, and wilt give ear to his commandments, and keep all his statutes, I will put none of these diseases upon thee, which I have brought upon the Egyptians: for I am the LORD that healeth thee. (Ex. 15:26)*

Common Connection

Today, we understand our healing is not based on the Old Testament covenant, but in the new covenant of grace. Doing right in God's sight is based in the obedience of Christ Jesus, not our obedience. However, the common connection we have with Hezekiah and Moses is we believe in God's Word above all else.

> *Who hath believed our report? and to whom is the arm of the LORD revealed? (Is. 53:1)*

Believing the Word in its entirety is the criteria for receiving all God's blessings. Some believers pick and choose aspects of His work on the cross by what their church doctrine upholds. Don't stop with theology. Allow the Word to develop your belief. It is the work of the Spirit through the written Word who produces the faith in our hearts. Keep hearing the Gospel for yourself. It is here that faith to believe in Jesus and what He purchased on the cross is birthed.

> *So faith cometh by hearing, and hearing by the word of God. (Rom. 10:17)*

Healing for All

Let us take a leap into the New Testament. Jesus and his followers confirm the Father's stance regarding healing. From fevers, mental health disorders to paralysis, healing of all various diseases continues.

> *And his fame went throughout all Syria: and they brought unto Him all the sick people that were taken with divers diseases and torments, and those which were possessed with devils, and those which were*

lunatic, and those that had the palsy; and he healed them. (Matt. 4:24)

No reason to be a bystander, receive your own restoration. Hezekiah knew life had much more in store, so why not ask for a long and satisfying life too.

With long life will I satisfy him, and shew him my salvation. (Ps. 91:16)

Day 33

Don't Fear Your Failure

Fear is an evil enemy. It captures minds and breaks your crown of peace. As in the days of Jeremiah, Israel became a slave rather than His servant carrying out His glory to the nations. When God's people forsook the living water of Christ, they became like broken cisterns, holding no water. Have you too experienced a drought in your walk with the Lord?

> *For my people have committed two evils; they have forsaken me the fountain of living waters, and hewed them out cisterns, broken cisterns, that can hold no water. Is Israel a servant? is he a homeborn slave? why is he spoiled? (Jer. 2:13-14)*

Forgetting the Father, the Israelites swung their own doors open to fear. No longer listening to their loving Lord, they instead heard roaring lions savaging their land. Their backsliding left them with broken crowns upon their head.

The young lions roared upon him, and yelled, and they made his land waste: his cities are burned without inhabitant. Also the children of Noph and Tahapanes have broken the crown of thy head. Hast thou not procured this unto thyself, in that thou hast forsaken the LORD thy God, when he led thee by the way? Thine own wickedness shall correct thee, and thy backslidings shall reprove thee: know therefore and see that it is an evil thing and bitter, that thou hast forsaken the LORD thy God, and that my fear is not in thee, saith the Lord GOD of host. (Jer. 2:15-17,19)

Can we, like the Israelites, instigate roaring lions to trample over our lives? We must be honest with ourselves, sometimes the portal into our problems has been due to our personal backsliding. Whether or not our choices have removed our peace, God still holds open the window of grace. He never stops extending his scepter of forgiveness. We serve a God of pardon.

Who is a God like unto thee, that pardoneth iniquity, and passeth by the transgression of the remnant of his heritage? he retaineth not his anger for ever, because he delighteth in mercy. (Micah 7:18)

Slide back into the loving arms of Jesus Christ. He will tell you not to fear your failure. Now take up your sword and tread upon the lions causing you despair. You can't lose your kingly position because Jesus has crowned you with His everlasting glory.

> *Thou shalt tread upon the lion and adder: the young lion and the dragon shalt thou trample under feet. (Ps. 91:13)*
>
> *In that day shall the LORD of hosts be for a crown of glory, and for a diadem of beauty, unto the residue of his people. (Is. 28:5)*

Concluding Thoughts

> *The light of the body is the eye: if therefore thine eye be single, thy whole body shall be full of light. (Matt. 6:22)*

The eye is like a lamp, illuminating our decisions and directing our paths. Keeping the eye cleared from confusion permits our entire body to be filled with Christ Jesus. It is when we keep our eyes on the Lord, our lives are in harmony with the Heavenly Kingdom. Alignment with the Father's will means we will lack no good thing. With sins forgiven, even our bodies possess the power of Christ. Should this not mean we can be made whole, disease free, healed, and sound minded?

Keep a Single Eye

A single eye discards the risk of developing a double mind and heart. May we keep doubt from clouding our vision of Christ. This is possible when God's Word is our guiding light. The Word will cleanse our doubts and create saving faith. Faith is a gift which seals the Father's Kingdom inside our hearts. Now may we live by faith and believe all fear is left outside Heaven's Gate!

> *A double minded man is unstable in all his ways. (James 1:8)*

> *Draw nigh to God, and he will draw night to you. Cleanse your hands, ye sinners; and purify your hearts, ye double minded. (James 4:8)*

> *This is none other but the house of God, and this is the gate of heaven. (Gen. 28:17)*

> *I am the door: by me if any man enter in, he shall be saved, and shall go in and out, and find pasture. (Jn. 10:9)*

> *Thy kingdom come. Thy will be done, as it is in heaven. (Matt. 6:10)*

About the Author

Theresa Ellison has served in the capacity of hospice/hospital chaplain, bereavement coordinator, mental health therapist and alcohol/drug counselor. Currently, Theresa is dedicated to writing a Biblical perspective on how God's grace includes freedom from living in fear and grief. When she is not writing, Theresa is studying the Holy Bible and Hebrew.

Born and raised in the beautiful Upper Peninsula of Michigan, Theresa has always loved outdoor sports. She has settled along Minnesota's Northshore with her husband, Steve and German Shepherd, Remi. While they enjoy their visits with their children, they fill their empty nest by rescuing German Shepherds.

website: www.blessmyblog.com

Leaving Grief at Heaven's Gate: Sorrow No More: God's Grace Reigns Over Grief. Xulon Press 2020

Further Reading

Leaving Grief at Heaven's Gate, by Theresa Ellison, Xulon Press, Amazon, Barnes & Noble, Apple Books

Author's website: www.blessmyblog.com